NBA

NBA

Basketball

AN OFFICIAL
FAN'S GUIDE

MARK
VANCIL
& DON
JOZWIAK

Benchmark
PRESS

THIS IS A CARLTON BOOK

Published in the United States by
Benchmark Press
601 South LaSalle Street, Suite 500
Chicago, Illinois 60605

First published in the United Kingdom in 1998 by
Carlton Books Limited

10 9 8 7 6 5 4 3 2 1

ISBN 1-892049-05-8

Project editor: Martin Corteel
Project art editor: Paul Messam
Production: Sarah Schuman

Printed and bound in Italy

This book is available in quantity at special discounts for your
group or organization. For further information, contact:

Benchmark Press
601 South LaSalle Street, Suite 500
Chicago, Illinois 60605
tel (312) 939-3330
fax (312) 663-3557

PREVIOUS PAGE: Utah's Karl Malone delivers a dunk in the 1998 NBA
Finals over Chicago's Scottie Pippen. However, in the final
analysis, it was the Bulls who finished on top winning their sixth
NBA Championship in eight years.

Authors' acknowledgments

MARK VANCIL
Special thanks to Jim O'Donnell and Jeanne Frederick for their
tireless research and attention to detail. And to the NBA's Diane
Naughton, Brian McIntyre, Terry Lyons, Jan Hubbard and Pete
Steber for their remarkable ability to bring compassion and support to their commitment to quality. To Martin Corteel at Carlton
Books for making the process so smooth and professional. And
finally, to my wife, Laura, for all the coffee and care. This project couldn't
have been done without all these people in place. My thanks.

DON JOZWIAK
Many thanks to Martin Corteel and David Ballheimer at Carlton
Books for their hard word and guidance. Thanks also to my mother,
father and sister for their support and love. And thanks especially
to my remarkable wife, Rebecca, for tolerating the mess I made
while working on this project and for providing encouragement
every step of the way—I couldn't have done it without you.

Photo credits

The publishers would like to thank the following sources for their
kind permission to reproduce the pictures in this book:

©NBA Photos/Bill Baptist; NBA/Andrew D. Bernstein;
NBA/Nathaniel S. Butler; NBA/Lou Capozzola; NBA/Paul
Chapman; NBA Chris Covatta; NBA/Scott Cunningham;
NBA/Sam Forencich; NBA/Steven Freeman; NBA/Barry Gossage;
NBA/Don Grayston; NBA/Andy Hayt; NBA/Ron Hoskins;
NBA/Glenn James; NBA/Mitchell Layton; NBA /David Liam
Kyle; NBA/Brad Mangin; NBA/Fernando Medina; NBA/Mike
Moore; NBA/Layne Murdoch; NBA/Patrick Murphy-Racey;
NBA/Tim O'Dell; NBA/Dick Raphael; NBA/Jeff Reinking;
NBA/Noren Trotman; NBA/Rocky Widner; NBA/Steve
Woltman.

Every effort has been made to acknowledge correctly and contact
the source and/or copyright holder of each picture, and Carlton
Books Limited apologises for any unintentional errors or omis-
sions which will be corrected in future editions of this book.

CONTENTS

INTRODUCTION

On and off the court and all around the globe, the evolution of the NBA now seems more like a revolution.

A game once confined to a small group of major American cities and carried most often via radio, now reaches into 27 major markets in the United States and two more in Canada, with television providing action to more than 160 countries around the world.

Franchises have been added in Toronto and Vancouver and NBA players, once banned from international competition, captured the imagination of fans from Spain to Australia, Japan to South Africa as Dream Team III dominated at the Atlanta Olympics.

When NBA Commissioner David Stern visited China, officials asked him to bring the "Red Oxen," or the Chicago Bulls as they are known in the U.S. When he spoke with government leaders in Russia they asked about playing an NBA game in Red Square. When the league decided to take the game international, season-opening games were played in Japan.

Indeed, the game and its players have caused a stir well beyond the traditional boundaries of North America.

After veteran stars such as George Mikan, Wilt Chamberlain, Jerry West, Bill Russell, Oscar Robertson and Elgin Baylor carried the league through the 1950s and 1960s, a whole new wave of talent took over and set the stage for an unprecedented explosion in worldwide interest.

Julius Erving became one of the first players to stretch the imagination with his performances. His high-flying style and acrobatic dunks helped "Dr. J" establish a whole new standard for the next generation of players.

They must have been paying attention because the 1980s proved to be the dawn of a new age. Larry Bird and Magic Johnson came into the league together and landed with tradition-rich franchises in Boston and Los Angeles, respectively.

Next came Michael Jordan, who turned Chicago, yet another major media market, into an NBA power. Then Patrick Ewing, the 7–0 center with a soft jump shot, went to the New York Knicks, whose history matches that of the league itself.

Other stars such as Charles Barkley, Dominique Wilkins, Chris Mullin, Scottie Pippen, Hakeem Olajuwon and David Robinson joined in and helped turn the NBA game into a non-stop show.

Major television contracts brought the NBA to more homes than ever, widening the audience to viewers in virtually every country of the world. NBA arenas turned into miniature theme parks, each with its own attractions, and attendance for regular season games exploded.

Most importantly, the players didn't disappoint. Bird's Boston Celtics and Johnson's Los Angeles Lakers spent much of the 1980s fighting off challengers for NBA Championships. Then came the Detroit Pistons of Isiah Thomas and, finally, Jordan's Chicago Bulls, who reeled off three consecutive titles.

The players became some of the most recognizable athletes in the history of professional sports, their exploits and personalities making the NBA experience as great off the court as on.

And as the 1980s gave way to the '90s,

Shaquille O'Neal serves up a slam.

Whether it's a one-handed jam or a blocked shot, few players have the intimidating inside presence of Miami's Alonzo Mourning.

the league's popularity continued to grow. The generation of stars from the first Dream Team in 1992, like Magic and Bird, passed the torch on to a new generation of players such as Shaquille O'Neal, Anfernee Hardaway, Grant Hill and Allen Iverson. The revolution rolls on.

This transition was made smooth by the ongoing dominance of Jordan's Bulls. Despite a brief retirement that lasted less than two seasons, His Airness has led Chicago to six NBA Championships in eight years in the 1990s. Jordan has also given basketball fans around the world the chance to see a living legend every time he takes the court.

Despite the Bulls dynasty, there are many challengers to Jordan's throne. Who will dethrone the champs? Maybe some seasoned veterans, like Utah's Karl Malone and John Stockton or Houston's Barkley and Olajuwon, will summon a last charge at glory. Or perhaps a young gun, like Miami's Alonzo Mourning or Detroit's Hill, will break through and forge a new chapter in the league's history.

With the speed and quickness of a guard and the scoring ability of a small forward, David Robinson has redefined the center position. At 7–1, Robinson is a force at both ends of the floor.

5

THE HISTORY OF THE NBA

It all started with a peach basket and a round ball more than 100 years ago. But in the decades since Dr. James Naismith created the first rough version of basketball, the National Basketball Association has become home to the greatest players in the history of the game. From the NBA's first great big man, George Mikan, to the Boston Celtics dynasty and the great 1980s and '90s run of Larry Bird, Magic Johnson, Isiah Thomas and Michael Jordan, the league has become an international show and one of the most popular spectator sports of all time.

The Birth of a League

Dr. James Naismith couldn't have known that his simple idea would lead to the creation of a game played around the globe by some of the most gifted athletes sports had ever seen.

In 1891, Dr. Naismith had two peach baskets nailed to a gymnasium balcony at the Springfield Young Men's Christian Association Training School. Dr. Naismith was hoping to create an indoor activity during the cold winter months, and by hanging the baskets high off the ground he sought to promote finesse and agility over mere size and strength.

In less than 50 years, however, the game came to revolve around players with a variety of all-around skills. And by the spring of 1946, the beginnings of the NBA were firmly in place. Although college basketball dominated the interest of fans in America, the professional game started coming together. Though teams had been organized and playing for nearly 40 years, the level of interest rarely extended beyond the team's immediate geographical area.

The Basketball Association of America was no different, at least in its first season in 1946–47. There were 11 teams divided into two divisions, the Western and Eastern, and they were situated in some of the

Dr. Naismith holds an early model basketball.

country's biggest cities, including Boston, New York, Chicago, Philadelphia, Detroit and Cleveland. The league even had a franchise in Toronto.

The BAA also had a legitimate star in "Jumpin'" Joe Fulks, a 6–5 forward from Kentucky. At a time when no team was averaging as many as 80 points a game, Fulks was a sensation. Fulks was the only player to average more than 17 points a game as he led the BAA with a 23.2 points per game average during the league's inaugural season.

The BAA ran into immediate problems. By the start of the league's second season only seven teams remained. Baltimore eventually was added to even the divisions, but problems persisted and no one was sure whether a professional basketball league, particularly in a climate dominated by the college style and game, could flourish. The concept needed help at virtually every turn. Six of the eight BAA teams were in the East, which shut out most of the rest of the country. And while Fulks and Max Zaslofsky were legitimate stars, the league needed a high profile draw.

The BAA got significant boosts on both fronts

starting with the 1948–49 season when four teams from the National Basketball League, which operated primarily in the Midwest, joined forces with the BAA. Suddenly, the BAA had some of the highest profile players in some of the best basketball markets in the country.

THE NBA BEGINS

And, perhaps as important as anything that had happened to date in professional basketball, the BAA had George Mikan.

The BAA changed its name to the the National Basketball Association for the 1949–50 season when the surviving teams from the National Basketball League merged with the BAA. The league, rugged and prone to fouls because of some of its early rules, continued to fight through its problems as

• •

Bob Cousy (right) was one of the greatest point guards in NBA history.

more and more stars emerged. The game itself needed refinement. The first move in that direction came prior to the 1954–55 season when owners from the nine remaining NBA teams adopted two radical, and equally important, rules changes.

Syracuse owner Danny Biasone had dabbled with the concept of putting a time limit on ball possession. The idea was to keep teams from stalling. Not only was the tactic boring, but it disrupted a game that revolved around scoring. Biasone arrived at 24 seconds by figuring teams normally average 60 shots a game. Thus, 120 shots divided into 2,880, the number of seconds in a 48-minute game, came out to 24. The idea caught on quickly. If the offensive team didn't get off a shot that hit the rim within 24 seconds of taking possession, the defensive team would be awarded possession of the ball. The other rule involved the number of fouls teams could commit in any one quarter. Now teams that committed more than six fouls in a quarter were penalized. Instead of shooting two free throws, opposing players would shoot three for every foul after the sixth one in a given period. Not only did it succeed in making fouling an expensive tactic to keep the opposition from scoring, but it helped keep the game moving.

Red Auerbach and the Boston Celtics Dynasty

Unlike modern teams, those of the late 1950s had virtually no scouting system in place to evaluate talent. When a team chose a college player in the draft, the coach or general manager making the choice many times had never seen the player play.

All of which underscores the brilliance of Arnold "Red" Auerbach. By the start of the 1956–57 season, the league had been reduced to eight franchises—Boston, Philadelphia, Syracuse and New York in the Eastern Division and Fort Wayne, Minneapolis, St. Louis and Rochester in the Western Division. Over the next four seasons, however, three of greatest players in history would join the league. The first of these was Bill Russell, a slender, 6–9 center who had turned the University of San Francisco into a national college power. In fact, San Francisco went two straight seasons without losing a single game. Back in Boston, Auerbach took notice. The

Celtics had led the NBA in scoring during the 1955–56 season, averaging 106 points a game. They had three solid scorers in guards Bill Sharman and Bob Cousy and forward Ed Macauley. The team also had the rights to 6–4 Cliff Hagan, whom Boston had drafted in 1953, and whose military commitment was coming to a close.

But Auerbach needed a rebounder and he needed the kind of defense Russell could provide. While the Celtics scored a lot of points, they also gave up plenty, 105.3 a game during the 1955–56 season.

That Russell would be tied up with the Olympics in Melbourne, Australia, until December didn't matter to Auerbach. He knew what he wanted even though not even Auerbach knew what he was getting.

So in a move that would impact the entire league for 13 seasons, Auerbach gambled. He agreed to send Macauley and the rights to Hagan, both future Hall

of Famers, to St. Louis for the right to draft Russell.

Almost as important to the Celtics' future was the addition of high scoring rookie Tom Heinsohn. Auerbach used Boston's regular pick to choose Heinsohn, who immediately stepped into the scoring void left by Macauley's departure. With All-Stars Cousy and Sharman out front, Heinsohn at forward and Russell in the middle, the Celtics were suddenly covered at all spots.

Though the first installment on Auerbach's winnings came immediately, no one knew what was ahead. The Celtics, with Russell at center, beat St. Louis 4–3 in the 1957 Finals with a dramatic 125–123 double overtime victory in Game 7 to claim their first NBA Championship.

A year later, however, St. Louis got even. Hagan and Macauley teamed with superstar Bob Pettit and the Hawks eliminated Boston 4–2 in the 1958 Finals.

Nothing of the sort would happen again for eight years. Not only was Russell more brilliant and driven to succeed than anyone imagined, but Auerbach continued to load the roster with stars.

Players such as Frank Ramsey, K.C. Jones, Sam Jones, Tom "Satch" Sanders, John Havlicek and Don Nelson carried Boston through a league maturing quickly.

Though Elgin Baylor, perhaps the most acrobatic scorer the league had seen to that point, arrived in Minneapolis in 1958, Wilt Chamberlain in Philadelphia in 1959 and Oscar Robertson in Cincinnati in 1960, the Celtics marched on.

The Men in Charge: Bill Russell and Red Auerbach led the Boston Celtics to eight straight championships.

EIGHT CONSECUTIVE CHAMPIONSHIPS

Auerbach, perhaps the greatest coach the league has ever known, proved equally brilliant behind the scenes. His ability to spot talent and blend diverse personalities into the Celtics system turned the Boston franchise into one of the greatest in all professional sports.

The Celtics averaged a remarkable 57.6 regular season victories during the eight-year championship run. Not once did Boston lose more than 26 games in any one season. And when it mattered most, the Celtics never lost.

When the 1960 Finals went to Game 7 against St. Louis, Boston responded with a 122–103 victory. When the 1962 Finals went to Game 7 against Los Angeles, which is where the Minneapolis franchise moved, Boston pulled out a 110–107 victory in overtime.

In fact, once the Celtics reached the playoffs they seemed to lift their game even higher. During the 1963–64 season, Robertson, who had developed into a remarkable all-around player, led Cincinnati to a 55–25 record, just four games behind Boston in the Eastern Division.

Once the playoffs started, however, Cincinnati didn't have a chance. In a 4–1 semifinal round blitzing, Boston beat the Royals by an average of almost 13 points a game.

The beat went on through the 1965–66 season. But the last Boston championship proved to be one of the most difficult and required every ounce of Auerbach's genius.

Philadelphia, with Chamberlain winning his seventh straight scoring title, had added rookie Billy Cunningham through the draft. Cunningham could run the floor, jump as well as anybody in the league and he knew how to score. The 76ers finally appeared to have enough guns to shoot down Russell's Celtics.

Indeed, Philadelphia finished the regular season with 11 straight victories to win the Eastern Division by a game, with Boston finishing second for the first time in 10 years. The immediate result was that the Celtics had to play a first-round playoff series against Cincinnati while the 76ers rested.

Boston fought through a tough five-game series and was battle-tested, if not rested, when it met Philadelphia in the Eastern Division Finals. Whatever the reason, the 76ers fell apart. Boston dusted off Philadelphia 4–1 and coasted into the Finals against a Los Angeles Lakers team it had beaten before.

Still, the Celtics struggled. Auerbach had announced early in the season that his coaching career would end following the 1966 playoffs. He had not announced a replacement and early in the NBA Finals no one seemed very interested in Auerbach's successor.

But after the Celtics were upset at home in the first game of the Finals, Auerbach decided to let the world in on a secret of historic magnitude. Auerbach announced that Russell would become the first black head coach in NBA history when he took over coaching duties at the start of the 1966–67 season.

The stunning announcement had an uplifting effect on the Celtics. They beat Los Angeles three straight games and eventually held off the Lakers in a tough Game 7 for the franchise's eighth straight championship.

DYNASTY ENDS

Though the Boston dynasty would carry on after a one-year lapse, the end was clearly in sight. Auerbach moved to the Celtics' front office and the roster he had created was beginning to show its years.

Boston finished eight games behind Philadelphia in the Eastern Division in 1967–68 only to rally past the 76ers in the playoffs and win another NBA championship.

But in 1969, the last breaths of dynasty were there for all to see. And with the American Basketball Association heading into its second full season, changes were on the horizon. Nowhere was that more apparent than in Boston. The Celtics' regulars averaged 31 years of age, with Sam Jones nearly 36 and Russell 35 when the playoffs started.

The Celtics had finished back in fourth in the Eastern Division behind the Baltimore Bullets, Philadelphia 76ers and New York Knicks. These three teams had the fire of youth while Boston continued the fight with reputation and sheer intensity.

In Baltimore, rookie center Wes Unseld made one of the league's most dramatic debuts. He averaged 13.8 points and 18.2 rebounds and led the Bullets to the Eastern Division title. Although standing just 6–7, Unseld's body was packed with 245 pounds of solid muscle.

Combined with unusual mental toughness, Unseld immediately established himself as a presence under the basket, and Baltimore as a force to be reckoned with, which is why Unseld received both the Most Valuable Player and Rookie of the Year awards in 1969.

In New York, the Knicks were coming together quickly thanks to another undersized center, Willis Reed. With flashy Walt Frazier at guard, steady Bill Bradley at forward and Dick Barnett occupying the point, the Knicks were one of the league's best all-around teams. And they became significantly better after trading for forward Dave DeBusschere midway through the 1968–69 season. The Knicks, as it turned out, were only a season away from taking over where the Celtics left off.

Philadelphia, led by Cunningham, Hal Greer and Chet Walker remained solid as well. So, as the aging Celtics walked softly into the 1969 playoffs, the NBA's past, as well as its future, was there for all the world to see.

But the last gasp of champions proved to be just enough. Boston knocked off Philadelphia 4–1 in the semifinals, New York 4–2 in the Eastern Conference Finals and, matched once more against the Los Angeles Lakers, rolled into the NBA Finals.

Though the Lakers had Chamberlain this time, nothing changed. The Celtics came back from an early 2–0 deficit and won the deciding Game 7 by a single basket. The 11th championship in 13 years was the last for Russell, who retired as player and gave up the coaching reins at the same time.

"He was the greatest defensive player I have ever seen," states current Chicago General Manager Jerry Krause. "A lot of people say Russell couldn't play in today's game. A lot of people don't know Russell. He would have found a way. He knew how to win. And he would have found a way to adapt."

To this day, there are few players in the NBA who measure up to Russell as a combination of individual talent and team skills. He rebounded like Dennis Rodman and blocked shots like Dikembe Mutombo, and while he wasn't known as an offensive powerhouse, he found a way to score. Among the current generation of players, Russell would deserve comparisons to Michael Jordan, Magic Johnson and Larry Bird as superstars who elevated their teams to new heights.

The 1970s—The Changing of the Guard

After years of dominance by Boston in particular and the Eastern Division in general, the balance of power shifted almost annually during the 1970s. Eight different teams won championships including Seattle and Portland. The Los Angeles Lakers ended a run of futility in the Finals by winning one title while New York and Boston captured two apiece. Off the court, the American Basketball Association ceased operations in the middle of the decade with four teams joining the NBA.

Although the New York Knicks, coached by Red Holzman, took the decade's first championship, the biggest story of the season unfolded in Milwaukee.

Prior to the 1969–70 season, the Bucks and Phoenix Suns flipped a coin to determine the first pick in the 1969 NBA Draft. The coin flip had become an annual event between the two worst teams in the league, one each from the Western and Eastern Divisions.

But this one became one of the most important in basketball history. Lew Alcindor, or Kareem Abdul-Jabbar as he would be known later, had been one of the greatest players in college history at UCLA. With an unstoppable "sky-hook" and unusual agility given his slender 7–2 frame, Abdul-Jabbar was considered likely to become professional basketball's next dominant player.

Milwaukee won the flip and the NBA rights to Abdul-Jabbar. After the ABA failed to come up with a suitable financial package, Abdul-Jabbar agreed to sign with the Bucks. His impact, as expected, was immediate. He finished second in scoring (28.8) and third in rebounding (14.5) while lifting Milwaukee from 27 to 56 victories in his first season.

"He was an incredible player from the minute he joined the league," says former NBA player and coach Kevin Loughery. "There wasn't anything he couldn't do. And he had that shot that no one could stop."

The Knicks meanwhile had put together a team as fundamentally sound as any in history. Smart, disciplined, versatile and focused, New York had the league's best record and went on to record the franchise's first championship with a rousing seven-game Finals victory over the Lakers.

A year later Oscar Robertson, who had failed to win a single title during his brilliant career in Cincinnati, joined Milwaukee and provided all the help Abdul-Jabbar needed. The Bucks won a stunning 66 games during the regular season and breezed through the playoffs.

Boston, after a down period following Russell's retirement, came back strong starting with the 1971–72 season. The Celtics had players such as John Havlicek, Jo Jo White, Dave Cowens and Don Chaney leading yet another Eastern Division charge.

THE GREATEST SEASON

But no team could stop the last, and one of the greatest, runs put together by Chamberlain's 1971–72 Los Angeles Lakers. At 35, Chamberlain was now more of a defender and rebounder. The Lakers' offense revolved around sharpshooting guards Gail Goodrich and veteran Jerry West; Happy Hairston and Jim

McMillian, solid players, manned the forward spots, and the bench included future coach Pat Riley.

For all the dominance displayed by Boston during the 1960s and Milwaukee during the previous season, nothing could compare to Los Angeles' record-shattering assault.

They won an NBA-record 33 straight games during one stretch and finished 69–13 during the regular season. The Lakers were so dominant that they won by an average of more than 12 points a game while leading the league in scoring (121.0).

The playoffs weren't much different. Los Angeles had lost seven times in the championship round in nine years before 1972. Matched against the New York Knicks, that string stopped quickly. The Lakers knocked off New York 4–1 for the franchise's first title since the team moved from Minneapolis in 1960.

Over in the ABA, the league had discovered the one player who would eventually become its savior. After his junior season at the University of Massachusetts, Julius Erving was signed by the Virginia Squires. Erving became an instant sensation, averaging 27.3 points and 15.7 rebounds a game.

But it was not what Erving did as much as the flash and flair of the process. His dunks were thundering and came from everywhere. He slammed on the run, under the basket and over everyone, including 7–2 Kentucky center Artis Gilmore.

Though the ABA and NBA continued to talk about a merger, Erving would be the one player to eventually push the process forward.

Back in the NBA, the Boston Celtics were once again riding high in the East. Led by Havlicek's scoring and Dave Cowens' aggressive play in the middle, Boston averaged a league-high 59 victories from the start of the 1971–72 season through the 1976 Finals.

But unlike their predecessors, these Celtics didn't always get it done in the playoffs. During the five-season sprint Boston reached the Finals only twice, winning in 1974 and 1976.

• •

LEFT Kareem Abdul-Jabbar.
RIGHT Wilt Chamberlain rises above the crowd.

EXPANSION

The league, loaded with talent, expanded to 18 teams for the 1974–75 season, adding New Orleans, which would later become the Utah Jazz. More importantly, the power was distributed evenly among a handful of teams.

The Chicago Bulls, coached by Dick Motta, remained one of the league's toughest defensive teams. The Buffalo Braves, with high-scoring Bob McAdoo, improved to 49 victories while the Washington Bullets, with Elvin Hayes on board, were the East's best team.

But out West, three teams had emerged. Golden State, with Rick Barry back in the fold, won the Pacific Division and put together a brilliant postseason run that took the Warriors all the way to the Finals.

Right behind them, however, were Seattle and Portland. The SuperSonics were slowly building toward a title run of their own later in the decade while the Trail Blazers had won the 1974 coin flip for center Bill Walton.

Golden State's title romp past Washington only delayed the Bullets' own championship. After Boston won in 1976, Portland, Washington and Seattle followed with championships.

Off the court, the last major piece of business was finally resolved when four ABA teams—Denver, Indiana, New York and San Antonio—were admitted into the NBA prior to the 1976–77 season. It seemed only fitting that as the NBA celebrated its 30th season the ABA would be suffering through the last of its problems. The NBA started the 1976–77 season with 22 teams and a whole new group of potential stars.

A controversial trade landed Erving in Philadelphia, while Denver had David Thompson, the first No. 1 draft pick to ever sign with the ABA, and Dan Issel. San Antonio had high-scoring George "Iceman" Gervin and high-flying Larry Kenon and Indiana had high-scoring Billy Knight.

The Trail Blazers appeared to be on the verge of a dynasty thanks to Walton's presence. But the oft-injured center, who had been compared to everyone from Abdul-Jabbar to Russell, stayed healthy long enough for only a single championship.

With Walton controlling the middle offensively and defensively, Portland rallied to knock off Julius Erving's Philadelphia 76ers

SHINING STARS

Though four teams ultimately moved from the ABA to the NBA, the biggest winners proved to be basketball fans.

Now, for the first time, fans all over the country were able to see players like Julius Erving, 7–2 center Artis Gilmore, 6–4 scoring machine David Thompson, Dan Issel, Larry Kenon and George Gervin, a smooth-scoring 6–7 guard.

All of those former ABA players had an immediate impact on the NBA. Erving helped Philadelphia to the Atlantic Division title in 1977 while Thompson and Issel keyed Denver's Midwest Division title.

Individually, Indiana's Billy Knight finished second in scoring, Thompson fourth, Gervin ninth and Issel 10th in their first NBA season. Gilmore ranked fourth in rebounds while Indiana's Don Buse led the NBA in assists.

A year later, Gervin and Thompson finished first and second in scoring in one of the most dramatic head-to-head competitions in history. As if in memory of the old ABA and its high-flying, wide-open game, Thompson and Gervin decided the scoring title on the final day.

Thompson made his bid with a brilliant, 73-point performance in an afternoon game. Later that night, Gervin— needing 59 points—scored 63 to win the title, 27.21 ppg to 27.15.

for the 1977 crown.

Seattle and Washington, both led by veteran talent, closed out the decade by meeting back-to-back in the 1978 and 1979 Finals with the Bullets winning the first round and the SuperSonics the second.

With those championships, however, came the end of an era. The next decade would be defined by spectacular worldwide growth off the court and the brilliant play of a whole new generation of players on the court.

Julius Erving in his ABA days with the Squires. (right) Magic Johnson.

The Greatest Show On—
And Off—Earth

It all started where it had all started before. Red Auerbach, using a rule that would later be eliminated, selected 6–9 forward Larry Bird as a "junior eligible" in 1978. A year later, the Los Angeles Lakers won the 1979 coin flip and selected 6–9 guard Earvin "Magic" Johnson with the No. 1 pick in the draft. Once again, the league's premier franchises were headed into a decade-long battle with two of the greatest players in history leading the charge. By 1985, the NBA found itself positioned for the most lucrative period of its history. Michael Jordan landed in Chicago and Patrick Ewing in New York, giving the league superstars in its four major markets. The game would never be the same.

The twist and turn of an entire league's future fortunes hung on the flip of a coin in 1979.

By the end of the 1970s, the NBA found itself dominated by secondary markets. The Seattle SuperSonics won the 1979 championship, with Washington, San Antonio and Kansas City winning the other three divisions. The major media centers had dropped back in the pack with Chicago finishing last in the Midwest Division, New York and Boston fourth and fifth, respectively, in the Atlantic and Los Angeles third in the Pacific.

Over the next five seasons, however, luck and Red Auerbach's genius would go a long way toward changing all that.

Boston's Auerbach, as he had done time and again over the previous 30 years, made two moves that transformed the Celtics from a troubled franchise with a dark future into an instant contender.

Coming off a 32–50 season in 1978, Auerbach decided to use the Celtics' first-round draft pick, No. 6 overall, on a 6–9 forward at Indiana State University. Auerbach, invoking a rarely used rule, selected Larry Bird as a junior eligible. Bird had transferred to Indiana State early in his college career, so while his original college class graduated 1978, Bird still had a year of collegiate playing eligibility remaining.

Auerbach didn't care. As with Russell back in the 1950s, Auerbach saw something special in Bird. So while Bird stayed in school for another season, the Celtics limped to a 29–53 record during the 1978–79 season.

But the gamble paid off. Bird arrived for the 1979–80 season after one of the most widely watched college championship games in history. Bird led Indiana State into the NCAA championship game opposite Earvin "Magic" Johnson's Michigan State team.

With many highly talented teammates to back him up, Johnson cruised past Bird to the 1979 national championship. It proved to be only the beginning of an often brilliant, decade-long battle played out across the entire country.

THE CELTICS AND LAKERS RISE AGAIN

The Los Angeles Lakers, thanks to a previous trade that gave them Utah's first-round selection, won the annual coin flip for the NBA Draft's first pick and took Johnson. Boston then signed Bird and the league's two most storied franchises were back in business.

Very big business.

The coast-to-coast rivalry gave the league a boost no one could have expected. Bird and Johnson had captured the imagination of a nation during college and now they would carry on as professionals in environments perfectly suited to their respective styles. Bird, almost fundamentally perfect, was the ideal match for Boston's proud tradition built on fundamental concepts. As for Johnson, he had a nickname and a personality made for the high glitz Hollywood atmosphere that surrounded Lakers games.

Magic became "the man" in Los Angeles and the Lakers, with legendary Kareem Abdul-Jabbar in the middle, were now a team for the ages.

With the addition of two marquee names in the same season, particularly in Boston and Los Angeles, interest in the league exploded. And the players didn't disappoint.

The Lakers won the first championship of the Magic era with a dramatic Game 6 victory over Philadelphia in 1980. Johnson, forced to play center after Abdul-Jabbar was injured in Game 5, scored 42 points, grabbed 15 rebounds and handed out seven assists in a stunning 123–107 victory over the 76ers and Julius Erving at Philadelphia.

While Johnson had been solid during the regular season, nothing marked his legend like that championship performance. Bird, however, edged Johnson for Rookie of the Year by leading the Celtics to a 61–21 record and a Division title.

"Magic was the only player who could take three shots and still dominate a game," Erving said later.

Indeed, Magic and Bird went on to dominate the first half of the decade, with the Celtics winning their first title in 1981. And once more, Auerbach was in the middle of it all.

Prior to the season, Auerbach sent the No. 1 pick in the draft, which the Celtics had acquired in a trade, plus the No. 15 choice to Golden State for center Robert Parish and rights to the No. 3 pick, which turned out to be Kevin McHale. With Cedric Maxwell occupying the forward spot opposite Bird, Boston rolled.

The Celtics rallied past Philadelphia in the Eastern Conference Finals before dismissing Houston for the 1981 title.

TWO GREAT TEAMS

For Bird and Johnson, the real showdown didn't come until 1984. Erving's 76ers, including center Moses Malone, made back-to-back Finals appearances in 1982 and 1983 against the Lakers, with each team gaining a championship.

But it was the 1983–84 season that really kick-started professional basketball into a whole new gear. The high-scoring Denver Nuggets, coached by Doug Moe, led the league in scoring by averaging an amazing 123.7 points per game. Included in the Nuggets' season-long sprint was one of the more remarkable games in NBA history.

Matched against the Detroit Pistons, Denver scored 184 points and still managed to lose. The Pistons, led by Isiah Thomas, scored 186 and won in triple overtime in the highest scoring game of all time.

Elsewhere, the heavyweight bout everyone wanted to see slowly started to form. Boston breezed through the Eastern Conference and the Lakers did the same in the West.

For the first time since college, Bird and Johnson faced one another with a championship on the line as the 1984 Finals unfolded. This time, however, Bird found a measure of revenge.

And he had plenty of help.

One more move by Auerbach solidified the roster and set the process in motion. The Celtics acquired guard Dennis Johnson, a defensive specialist and former All-Star, in a steal of a deal with Phoenix before the season.

The Lakers, having gained James Worthy in the 1982 NBA Draft, were just as loaded with talent. So when the two teams opened the Finals in Boston, the eyes of an international audience were fixed on them.

The series embodied all the elements that had turned the NBA into the hottest professional sports league in the world. The three-point shot, an ABA feature instituted prior to the 1979–80 season, proved to be an exciting weapon in crunch time.

There were blowout victories by both teams, two dramatic overtime games and an even more compelling Game 7 showdown inside fabled Boston Garden. When it ended, Bird was named the Finals' Most Valuable Player and the NBA, already expanding rapidly beyond the United States, hit another new high in fan interest.

THE JORDAN PHENOMENON

As it turned out, the 1984 Finals were only the beginning. Chicago, using the No. 3 pick in the 1984 Draft, selected Michael Jordan in a move that rocked the record books and changed history.

For the second straight season Houston gained the No. 1 pick in the draft and selected a center. This time, the Rockets landed Hakeem Olajuwon. With 7–4 Ralph Sampson arriving the previous season, Olajuwon completed the "Twin Towers" in Houston.

Meanwhile, Portland decided to gamble with the No. 2 choice. The Trail Blazers had Clyde Drexler on their roster and desperately needed a center. So instead of taking Jordan, Portland chose 7–1 center Sam Bowie, who had missed two entire college seasons with leg injuries. Unfortunately for the Trail Blazers, Bowie's problems weren't behind him. Bowie missed an average of nearly 55 games a season during his five years in Portland.

With Jordan, the Bulls couldn't have been happier. He pumped life into a franchise that was near collapse and turned the cold and empty Chicago Stadium into one of the loudest arenas in all of sports. He also helped turn the league into a marketing phenomenon.

Jordan's shoe and apparel deal with Nike established a whole new commercial presence for professional athletes. Jordan, unlike Bird, Johnson or Erving before him, had a personalized shoe that sold millions of pairs before the 1984–85 season ended.

Jordan finished third in the league in scoring behind New York's Bernard King and Bird, averaging 28.2 points. More importantly for the league, Jordan turned

"SHOWTIME" IN LOS ANGELES

Hollywood couldn't have made a better casting call. When the Los Angeles Lakers decided to change coaches 11 games into the 1981–82 season they called on Pat Riley, a former player and one of the most intense competitors the game had ever known.

Riley had been a teammate of Lakers General Manager Jerry West and was a reserve on the 1971–72 Lakers team that won 33 straight games. So Riley, like his star Magic Johnson, knew how to win.

With slicked-back hair, a wardrobe full of Italian suits and a style all his own, Riley became the perfect complement to Johnson's wide-eyed enthusiasm. Riley turned the Lakers into an end-to-end attack, the offense quickly becoming known as "Showtime" for all the points it scored.

When the roster changed later, Riley went back to a low-post attack utalizing Johnson and Kareem Abdul-Jabbar. The Lakers also played solid defense when it mattered most and executed with precision.

Riley left Los Angeles following the 1989–90 season, having guided the Lakers to four championships and seven trips to the Finals in eight years at the helm.

the Bulls into a wondrous road show despite an otherwise ragged roster.

The Bulls finished third in the Central Division and reached the playoffs for only the second time in eight years. Off the court, Jordan turned into a household name with major marketing and advertising deals covering everything from soft drinks to fast food and automobiles.

"He's the real thing, no question," said Kevin Loughery, Jordan's first NBA coach. "He understands the entire game, on and off the court. No one knows how good this kid is going to be. He's a killer. This guy will be one of the greatest players to ever play the game if he stays healthy."

Meanwhile another Lakers–Celtics championship showdown ended with the title going back to Los Angeles. But not for long.

The Celtics added the often-injured veteran center Bill Walton for the 1985–86 season and came within two games of the regular-season victory record. Boston finished 67–15 and roared into the Finals against Houston's towering frontline of 7–0 Olajuwon, 7–4 Sampson and 6–8 Rodney McCray.

First, however, Boston had to dismiss Jordan's pesky Bulls. Jordan had missed all but 18 games of the regular season due

Boston Celtics' Larry Bird.

to a broken foot. He returned for the first round of the playoffs and put on one of the greatest one-man shows in history.

Playing against the eventual champs with a thin supporting cast, Jordan bombed Dennis Johnson and the Celtics for 49 points in a Game 1 loss. Then, before a national television audience on a warm Sunday afternoon, Jordan exploded for 63 points and carried the Bulls into double overtime before the Celtics prevailed. Although Boston went on to sail through the Eastern Conference playoffs, Bird had seen more than enough of Jordan.

"Maybe it was God disguised as Michael Jordan," quipped Bird after the Game 2 scare, the highest scoring playoff performance in history.

THE LOTTERY

Houston's ability to land consecutive No. 1 picks led to the creation of the lottery for the 1985 Draft. And that's when the final piece of the puzzle fell in place for the NBA.

New York, the league's primary media market, had finished 23–59 and needed help. More specifically, the New York market needed a star. And they got one when the Knicks ended up with the No. 1 pick and landed 7–0 center Patrick Ewing.

For the league, the circle was virtually complete. With Johnson in Los Angeles, Bird in Boston, Jordan in Chicago and Ewing in New York, the NBA became an even more lucrative television draw. On the marketing side, the league was moving outside the United States and into countries all over the world with sales of league merchandise spiraling.

"This is the best game in sports," said former Bulls Coach Stan Albeck at the time. "You have everything. The game is fast, the players are incredibly skilled and going to an NBA arena is fun. The whole thing is entertainment."

It wasn't until the 1987–88 season that a slow changing of the guard started to take place. Detroit, with a tough and disciplined lineup keyed by Thomas, finally knocked

Boston out of the playoffs and reached the Finals. In terms of championships, the Bird era ended when the Pistons closed out the Eastern Conference Finals with a 4–2 decision over the Celtics in 1988.

Although Johnson helped the Lakers rally to a 4–3 victory over Detroit in the 1988 NBA Finals, it was his final championship as well. The Lakers became the first team since the Celtics in 1968 and 1969 to win consecutive championships. But the pages were turning. Kareem Abdul-Jabbar retired the following season after 20 brilliant seasons and 44,149 points.

"It couldn't have been any better," said Abdul-Jabbar. "Not when I can remember growing up on the streets of Manhattan and hoping I got to play one pro season. I outlasted everybody. I got to play with the greats of the game. I realized all my professional goals."

Nowhere was that more evident than in Detroit. Known for their rough and tumble defense, the Pistons, who swept the Lakers in four games in 1989 made a third straight trip to the Finals in 1990 after yet another bruising Eastern Conference playoff match with Jordan's Bulls.

With Thomas leading the Pistons' charge, Detroit knocked off Portland for a second straight championship. Like the Lakers before them, the Pistons felt they had left their mark by winning two in a row. But unlike the Lakers, the run came to a close quickly.

With solid support in Scottie Pippen, Horace Grant and Bill Cartwright and the steady leadership of Coach Phil Jackson behind him, Jordan guided the Bulls to the promised land in 1991. Chicago won 61 regular season games, a franchise record, and then marched through the playoffs and knocked off Johnson's Lakers 4–1 in the 1991 Finals. As it turned out, the league would never be the same. In a stunning development prior to the 1991–92 season, Johnson announced he had HIV and would retire from basketball.

Johnson, one of the classiest players sport had ever known, left with five rings and nine trips to the Finals. His smile and enthusiasm turned a game into entertainment and his ability had turned the Lakers into a remarkable end-to-end show.

"Describing Earvin Johnson is more complicated than one might guess because the man is more complicated than he at first seems," says Abdul-Jabbar. "The whole world knows about his sense of showmanship and his flair for the spectacular, but the inner man, the fierce competitor with the iron will to win, is often concealed by the smile and the easy demeanor."

As Johnson left the game, Bird limped on behind him. Though Boston remained among the East's strongest teams, Bird missed 45 games during the 1991–92 season because of a serious back injury.

THE BULLS' ERA

The future suddenly moved to Chicago. With Jordan winning his sixth straight scoring title and the roster staying healthy, the Bulls sprinted to a 67–15 regular-season record. But they didn't stop there. After rolling through the East on their way to the Finals, the Bulls upended Portland with a dramatic fourth-quarter comeback in Game 6 at Chicago Stadium.

"Can they win three in a row?" Magic Johnson considered the question. "They could, but I don't know," said Johnson. "If they thought winning two in a row was tough winning three is even harder. I know. I tried."

Johnson flirted with a comeback— he remained a key member of the gold medal-winning Dream Team, and Bird's sore back forced him to retire.

Phoenix pulled off a huge trade before the 1992–93 season, dealing three players to Philadelphia for Charles Barkley. The New York Knicks added Charles Smith and Glenn "Doc" Rivers, and coach Pat Riley, who had won four titles with the Lakers.

But Chicago continued to roll. Jordan won his seventh straight scoring title to match Wilt Chamberlain's league record. In the playoffs, Chicago defeated the Knicks to win the Eastern Conference title. In the 1993 Finals, Jordan again came through against Barkley, as Chicago became the first team in 27 years to win three consecutive titles.

Jordan then retired for 17 months and the balance of power shifted West. Barkley was in Phoenix, David Robinson in San Antonio, Drexler in Portland, Shawn Kemp

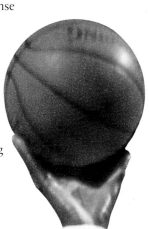

OPPOSITE Michael Jordan sails in for a monster slam. **BELOW** Hakeem Olajuwon lifts another jump hook.

in Seattle and Olajuwon in Houston. While many of those players had been in place for years, the real change came in their supporting casts. Nowhere was that more true than in Houston.

Matched against the rugged New York Knicks in the 1994 Finals, Houston became the first Western Conference team other than the Los Angeles Lakers to win the title since 1978. A year later, the Rockets—with Drexler coming on board in February 1995—became the first team to defeat four 50-win teams in one playoff and capped their title run with a four-game sweep of Orlando in the NBA Finals.

With Jordan back on top of his game in 1995–96, the Bulls embarked on one of the greatest seasons in the history of sports. Chicago's regular-season 72–10 record eclipsed the 69–13 mark posted by the 1971–72 Lakers. By the time the Bulls were done demolishing their competition in the playoffs, they had a combined 87–13 record for the regular season and playoffs. Jordan won a slew of awards: regular-season MVP, All-Star Game MVP and NBA Finals MVP—and a spot on the NBA All-Defense first team squad.

The 1996–97 and 1997–98 seasons weren't identical copies, but the end results were very similiar. The Bulls returned to the NBA Finals by outlasting their Eastern Conference opponents, while the Utah Jazz claimed the competitive Western Conference. The NBA Finals were six-game affairs, and the Bulls were left holding the championship trophy at the end. Despite fine performances by Jazz stars Karl Malone and John Stockton, Jordan won both the title and the NBA Finals MVP award each year.

The Chicago Bulls have dominated basketball in the 1990s. Is Jordan's team the best the NBA has ever seen, or does that honor belong to the Celtics of the '60s or the Lakers of the '80s? That's a topic fans can enjoy debating, but Jordan would like to answer the question— with an exclamation point—by adding even more championship rings to his collection.

THE NBA FINALS

YEAR	WINNER	SERIES	LOSER
1947	Philadelphia	4–1	Chicago
1948	Baltimore	4–2	Philadelphia
1949	Minneapolis	4–2	Washington
1950	Minneapolis	4–2	Syracuse
1951	Rochester	4–3	New York
1952	Minneapolis	4–3	New York
1953	Minneapolis	4–1	New York
1954	Minneapolis	4–3	Syracuse
1955	Syracuse	4–3	Fort Worth
1956	Philadelphia	4–1	Fort Worth
1957	Boston	4–3	St. Louis
1958	St. Louis	4–2	Boston
1959	Boston	4–0	Minneapolis
1960	Boston	4–3	St. Louis
1961	Boston	4–1	St. Louis
1962	Boston	4–3	Los Angeles
1963	Boston	4–2	Los Angeles
1964	Boston	4–1	San Francisco
1965	Boston	4–1	Los Angeles
1966	Boston	4–3	Los Angeles
1967	Philadelphia	4–2	San Francisco
1968	Boston	4–2	Los Angeles
1969	Boston	4–3	Los Angeles
1970	New York	4–3	Los Angeles
1971	Milwaukee	4–0	Baltimore
1972	Los Angeles	4–1	New York
1973	New York	4–1	Los Angeles
1974	Boston	4–3	Milwaukee
1975	Golden State	4–0	Washington
1976	Boston	4–2	Phoenix
1977	Portland	4–2	Philadelphia
1978	Washington	4–3	Seattle
1979	Seattle	4–1	Washington
1980	Los Angeles	4–2	Philadelphia
1981	Boston	4–2	Houston
1982	Los Angeles	4–2	Philadelphia
1983	Philadelphia	4–0	Los Angeles
1984	Boston	4–2	Los Angeles Lakers
1985	Los Angeles Lakers	4–2	Boston
1986	Boston	4–2	Houston
1987	Los Angeles Lakers	4–2	Boston
1988	Los Angeles Lakers	4–3	Detroit
1989	Detroit	4–0	Los Angeles Lakers
1990	Detroit	4–1	Portland
1991	Chicago	4–1	Los Angeles Lakers
1992	Chicago	4–2	Portland
1993	Chicago	4–2	Phoenix
1994	Houston	4–3	New York
1995	Houston	4–0	Orlando
1996	Chicago	4–2	Seattle
1997	Chicago	4–2	Utah
1998	Chicago	4–2	Utah

THE TEAMS

For all the individual demands, basketball has always revolved around the rhythm of a team. From the beginning the NBA has been identified by its teams, those great and those in pursuit of greatness.

The record books are full of names and numbers, superstars and stats. Individuals win scoring titles, rebounding titles and block all the shots. They pass out assists and lead the league in steals. But all of them operate within the context of a team. And the greatest of those teams — the Boston Celtics, Los Angeles Lakers and Chicago Bulls — managed to combine diverse individual talents into a singular battle plan.

In the 1950s, every NBA team chased the Minneapolis Lakers. But for all George Mikan's brilliance, not even he could have carried the Lakers to championship after championship by himself. When the Celtics came together under the guidance of Arnold "Red" Auerbach, they came together as a cohesive unit with stars at virtually every position. The Los Angeles Lakers, with Magic Johnson leading the charge in the 1980s, relied on a selfless approach that mirrored that of Auerbach's Celtics. Even with Michael Jordan, perhaps the greatest player to ever play the game, the Chicago Bulls didn't win a single title until Scottie Pippen, Horace Grant and others filled in around him. From East to West, NBA teams have fought to create their own history, each of them traveling the same road in search of championships.

Top teammates: Scottie Pippen and Michael Jordan.

ATLANTA HAWKS

Changing of the Guard

For many of its early NBA years, Atlanta was a franchise on the move. The Hawks played in Moline, Milwaukee and St. Louis before landing in Atlanta. The common thread in all those stops has been the presence of high-scoring forwards like Bob Pettit, Dominique Wilkins and Danny Manning. But now the Hawks rely on a pair of flashy guards, Mookie Blaylock and Steve Smith, and center Dikembe Mutombo.

Few NBA teams have had as many lives as the Atlanta Hawks. And few have had a more colorful past. Though blessed with a rich history that includes some of the league's most noted players and coaches—Arnold "Red" Auerbach coached the team for most of the 1949–50 season, its first in the NBA— Atlanta spent its early years moving through the Midwest in search of a home.

The Hawks made their NBA debut in 1949, coming from the old NBL as the Tri-City Blackhawks. They moved to Milwaukee two years later and coach Red Holzman, who became one of the most successful leaders in history while running the New York Knicks, came on and guided the Hawks through the first of many difficult transitions. Holzman started out as a play-

Mookie Blaylock soars over Scottie Pippen.

er/coach for the Hawks, but neither his playing nor his coaching could pull the team above the .500 mark.

Then the Hawks got a break. Though the struggle would continue, the 1954 NBA

Draft produced one of the game's greatest players. Bob Pettit, a brilliant scorer and perhaps the greatest forward of his era, arrived from Louisiana State University. Not even Pettit's star power, however, could keep fan interest in Milwaukee.

So owner Ben Kerner moved the Hawks, complete with Pettit and Holtzman, to St. Louis where the franchise flourished. But not before the Hawks participated in one of the most famous trades in NBA history. In April, 1956, the Hawks sent their first-round draft choice to Boston for Ed Macauley and Cliff Hagan. Though Macauley and Hagan became Hall of Famers, Boston ended up getting the better of the deal. That first-round pick ended up being Bill Russell, who would lead the Celtics to a remarkable 11 NBA titles.

And the first of those came at the expense of the Hawks. Boston beat St. Louis for the 1957 NBA title. But a year later, with Pettit leading the way, the Hawks won their first and only championship by downing Russell's Celtics. Boston would win the next eight titles while the Hawks remained strong, but never quite good enough.

The team eventually moved again, this time to Atlanta in 1968. The next great wave came in the mid 1980s when Dominique Wilkins, one of the most exciting players ever, became the team's leading scorer. Wilkins, combined with players such as Kevin Willis, Tree Rollins and Glenn "Doc" Rivers, led a spirited run during the mid and

ROLL OF HONOR

Conference/Division	Eastern/Central			
First NBA year	1949–50			
Home Arena details	Georgia Dome (built 1992, capacity 21,570)			
Former cities/nicknames	Tri-Cities Blackhawks (1949–51), Milwaukee Hawks (1951–55), St. Louis Hawks (1955–68)			
NBA Championships	1958			
Playing Record	**G**	**W**	**L**	**Pct**
Regular Season	3878	1950	1888	.513
Playoffs (Series 19–34)	259	114	145	.440

LENNY WILKENS
A Coach's Coach

Lenny Wilkens always played the game as if he were a coach on the court.

He displayed an ability to break down defenses as evidenced by a 15-year Hall of Fame career that included nine All-Star Game appearances. Wilkens was named player/coach at Seattle in 1969, and coached the team for three seasons.

Wilkens eventually continued his playing career at Cleveland and then Portland, where he again became player/coach before retiring as a player in 1975.

He returned to Seattle and led the Super-Sonics into the NBA Finals two consecutive seasons, the second of which produced the franchise's first championship in 1979.

Wilkens then moved to Atlanta where he established himself as the most successful coach in NBA history. Through the 1997–98 season, Wilkens' teams had won 1,120 games, 182 more than legendary Boston Coach Arnold "Red" Auerbach.

Wilkens received the ultimate reward in 1998 when he was elected to the Hall of Fame for the second time, this time as a coach.

late 1980s, but teams like Boston and Detroit kept them from the NBA Finals.

Coaching great Lenny Wilkens took the helm in 1993 and rebuilt the team in his image, with a team-oriented style based on outstanding guard play. Under his guidance, point guard Mookie Blaylock and shooting guard Steve Smith have become one of the NBA's top backcourt duos. The addition of versatile forward Christian Laettner and shot-blocking center Dikembe Mutombo gave Lenny Wilkens two quality big men to build the Hawks' future around.

Wilkens has surrounded his stars with a deep cast of role players, and the Hawks are able to adapt to nearly any style of play. Blaylock and Mutombo are the defensive keys to Atlanta's ability to shut down opposing scorers. Wilkens has helped the Hawks become a perennial playoff squad who are not far from being NBA title contenders.

Top Two: Steve Smith (left) and Mookie Blaylock.

Basketball's Greatest Franchise

No team in the history of professional sports in America dominated more completely than the Boston Celtics of the late 1950s and 1960s. With a legendary coach in Arnold "Red" Auerbach on the sidelines and Bill Russell, perhaps the greatest big man ever to play the game, playing center, the Celtics won 11 championships in 13 years including an NBA record eight straight. Boston has won more regular season games and postseason titles than any team in NBA history. Now Coach Rick Pitino faces the challenge of returning the Celtics to greatness.

By the time Arnold "Red" Auerbach turned over the day-to-day operations of the Boston Celtics, no one doubted the genius of the NBA's most successful coach.

He presided over the greatest dynasty in American professional sports history. His teams won nine championships including eight straight from 1959–66. But that is only part of his contribution to Boston's history.

His greatest attribute might have been making deals and evaluating talent. The first franchise-shaking move came before the 1956–57 season when Auerbach traded veterans Ed Macauley and Cliff Hagan to St. Louis for the Hawks' first-round pick in the 1956 Draft. The player Auerbach wanted was 6–10 center Bill Russell. He also picked

Dynamic Duo: Bill and "Red" celebrate!

K.C. Jones and made Tommy Heinsohn a territorial pick. A year later, Auerbach added shooting guard Sam Jones. These eventual Hall of Famers turned Boston into a dynasty. Auerbach continued to build the team through the draft. In 1962, following the

Celtics' fourth straight title, Boston selected John Havlicek in the first round.

In the summer of 1966, Auerbach turned the coaching duties over to Russell, who became the NBA's first black head coach. Russell's teams won two more titles in his three seasons in the dual role of player/coach.

Boston won two more titles in the 1970s with Heinsohn coaching a team dominated by Havlicek and Dave Cowens. But just as the Celtics appeared headed for an extended lull following a sub-.500 season in 1977–78, Auerbach made another round of moves that would define yet another era.

Auerbach used the team's first-round draft pick to take Larry Bird. It was a gutsy move, since Bird wasn't eligible to join the Celtics for a year. It was the second great move of Auerbach's career. Although Boston suffered another losing season waiting for Bird, his arrival was well worth the wait.

Auerbach then traded for Golden State center Robert Parish and the No. 3 pick overall, which Auerbach used to select Kevin McHale. Separate deals later landed guards Dennis Johnson and Danny Ainge, all of which made Boston the Eastern Conference's dominant team yet again in the early 1980s. The Bird era produced three championships and five more trips to the NBA Finals.

The Celtics have been dogged by misfortune since the mid-1980s. The second pick of the 1986 draft, Len Bias, died before playing a game. Bird then retired with back trou-

ROLL OF HONOR

Conference/Division	Eastern/Atlantic			
First NBA year	1946–47			
Home Arena details	FleetCenter (built 1995, capacity 18,600)			
Former cities/nicknames	None			
NBA Championships	1957, 1959, 1960, 1961, 1962, 1963, 1964, 1965,			
	1966, 1968, 1969, 1974, 1976, 1981, 1984, 1986			

Playing Record	G	W	L	Pct
Regular Season	4047	2472	1575	.611
Playoffs (Series 63–25)	461	272	189	.590

★ ★ ★ ★ ★ ★ ★ ★ ★ ★

RED AUERBACH
A Basketball Genius

If Arnold "Red" Auerbach had only coached, he would be remembered as one of the NBA's true legends.

But Auerbach did much more than that during a career that started in the 1940s and continues into the 1990s. As coach, then General Manager, Auerbach knew exactly the kind of player that could make it in the NBA.

Auerbach shipped two future Hall of Fame players to St. Louis for the rights to the Hawks' first pick in the 1956 Draft. Auerbach then used that pick to select Bill Russell, who would turn Auerbach's gamble into a monumental payoff.

With Auerbach coaching and managing the team's roster, Boston won nine NBA championships in 10 years, including a remarkable string of eight straight.

Auerbach moved to the front office following the 1965–66 season. But his moves helped produce seven additional championships.

And at the end of all of them, Auerbach could be found lighting a gigantic "victory cigar," which became as much a symbol of the Celtics' success as the man himself.

ble in 1992 and new team leader Reggie Lewis died during the summer of 1993.

In 1997, Auerbach brought in former Knicks and collegiate coach Rick Pitino to rebuild the Celtics. Pitino helped turn New York around when the Knicks were floundering, and then coached the University of Kentucky to the NCAA championship.

Pitino started rebuilding in Boston by instituting large-scale roster changes. When the dust settled, the Celtics were left with a versatile young squad. High-flying forwards Antoine Walker and Ron Mercer give the team an exciting frontcourt tandem, and veteran point guard Kenny Anderson was acquired to make sure they get the ball. Walker averaged a double-double in 1997–98, and as he continues to improve the Celtics are poised for a return to greatness with Pitino calling the shots and Auerbach watching over his shoulder—no doubt readying a few more victory cigars.

Antoine Walker takes to the sky.

The NBA's Buzz

Considered a long shot when the most recent expansion process started, Charlotte put together a solid plan and found itself with one of four new franchises. With smart marketing moves and even brighter player decisions, the Hornets have become one of the most successful young teams in the league. With underrated forward Glen Rice leading the way, no one doubts Charlotte now.

They came out of nowhere in 1988 and the Charlotte Hornets haven't stopped rolling since.

One of two franchises added to the league for the 1988–89 season, Charlotte made all the right moves immediately. On court, the Hornets moved patiently while building one of the league's best young teams. Off court, Charlotte became one of the NBA's most popular franchises by combining basketball success with brilliant marketing.

As a result, Charlotte led the league in attendance in four of its first five seasons. The 23,698-seat Charlotte Coliseum is one of the NBA's largest and loudest arenas, its fans packing the "Hive" for virtually every home game since the team arrived.

In its early days, the Hornets had a couple of reasons for all the noise and notice. One of those was All-Star forward Larry

Hornets center Vlade Divac hits a hook shot.

Johnson. A rugged rebounder and powerful scorer, Johnson became the team's first real pillar. Charlotte used the first pick in the 1991 draft to select Johnson from the University of Nevada-Las Vegas (UNLV). And he didn't disappoint.

Johnson quickly became recognized as one of the best power forwards in the league. He averaged more than 20 points and 10 rebounds in each of his first two seasons. Johnson was named NBA Rookie of the Year in 1992 and a year later was chosen to the All-NBA second team.

But Johnson couldn't get it done alone, and the Hornets struggled through their first four seasons. Then came Alonzo Mourning. Although Shaquille O'Neal gained more notoriety during the 1992–93 season, Mourning established himself as one of the best young centers to enter the NBA in years. The year before Mourning arrived, Charlotte had stumbled to a 31–51 record. Kenny Gattison, though a solid competitor, had been forced to play the middle despite standing just 6–8. Opposing teams had taken advantage, which forced Johnson to carry much of the offensive and defensive load. But all that changed with Mourning. The Hornets, under coach Allan Bristow, won 44 regular-season games to make the playoffs for the first time.

Charlotte more than passed its first playoff tests. The Hornets blew by Boston in the first round of the 1993 postseason and fought the powerful New York Knicks hard

R O L L   O F   H O N O R

Conference/Division	Eastern/Central			
First NBA year	1988–89			
Home Arena details	Charlotte Coliseum (built 1988, capacity 23,698)			
Former cities/nicknames	None			
NBA Championships	None			
Playing Record	G	W	L	Pct
Regular Season	820	377	433	.460
Playoffs (Series 2–4)	25	9	16	.360

before getting eliminated in the Eastern Conference Semifinals.

Injuries to Johnson and Mourning slowed the Hornets' progress after their playoff run in 1993. Johnson came back strong from his injuries in 1995, but Mourning found his days were numbered in a Hornets uniform and he was traded to Miami at the start of the 1995–96 season.

But, the deal netted them another star in Glen Rice, a small forward with seemingly endless three-point range. He played in his first All-Star Game after joining the Hornets, helping Charlotte fans to forget Mourning.

Fans also had to adjust to the loss of Johnson, who was traded to the Knicks for versatile forward Anthony Mason prior to the 1996–97 season. Mason—who has the size of a power forward, speed of a small forward and ball-handling skills of a guard—and Rice joined former Lakers center Vlade Divac as the new nucleus of the Hornets. Charlotte also signed former Celtics point guard David Wesley to run the offense. By the spring of 1997, Charlotte had just two players left from the Hornets' first days: Tyrone "Muggsy" Bogues, the NBA's shortest player at 5–3, and sweet-shooting reserve Dell Curry.

The Hornets also made a big change on the bench, hiring former Boston Celtics great Dave Cowens before the 1996–97 season. Cowens earned the respect of his team, then helped the Hornets earn the NBA's respect once again. Charlotte reeled off two consecutive 50-plus win seasons under Cowens, and the franchise enters its second decade with fans buzzing louder than ever.

Lift Off: Glen Rice soars through the air.

DAVE COWENS
Leading By Example

There is a theory that NBA players perform better for coaches who were once players themselves. That may explain why Dave Cowens became an immediate success as Charlotte's head coach.

Cowens learned about the game on the floor of the old Boston Garden. At 6–9 and 230 pounds, he was an undersized, over-achieving center for the Celtics. Cowens was a warrior under the boards, outrebounding bigger players. He helped Boston win NBA Championships in 1974 and '76. He stepped in as player/coach for the Celtics in 1978–79 after the team got off to a 2–12 start, guiding the team to a 27–41 mark over the rest of the season.

Cowens is a demanding coach, but he understands the pressures each player deals with during the season. Knowing which buttons to push has helped Cowens become one of the NBA's new coaching stars. If his Hall of Fame career as a player is any indication, Hornets fans may be seeing the start of something special in Charlotte.

CHICAGO BULLS

Rebuilding A Winner

With one of the game's greatest players in Michael Jordan, the Chicago Bulls became the first team in more than 25 years to win three straight NBA Championships. Jordan turned a struggling franchise into the dominant team of the early 1990s with a spectacular combination of style and substance that made the Bulls one of the best teams in league history. Following a brief time-out, Air Jordan has steered the Bulls to greatness.

The Chicago Bulls story is a tale of two eras, with defense the single thread connecting them.

When coach Dick Motta took over the Chicago Bulls in 1968, the franchise was was entering its third season. Johnny "Red" Kerr had guided the expansion Bulls into the playoffs in their first two seasons, but management decided it wanted a fresh young coach and hired Motta.

Within a year, Motta had built the offense around a pair of high-scoring forwards in Bob Love and Chet Walker. The defense revolved around Jerry Sloan, whose competitive intensity intimidated many opponents.

From 1970 to 1975, Chicago led the league in defense twice and never finished lower than third. They reached the Western Conference Finals in 1974 and 1975.

Look Up: Toni Kukoc dunks on the Phoenix Suns.

After Motta left in 1976, management acquired aging stars like Artis Gilmore and Larry Kenon. That didn't work, and they compounded the problem with poor draft choices. By 1984 the Bulls needed a savior.

They got three of them.

First, Michael Jordan arrived in the 1984 Draft. Then Jerry Reinsdorf bought the team midway through the 1984–85 season and inserted Jerry Krause as general manager. Krause, who had been a Bulls scout in the late 1960s and early 1970s knew exactly the kind of team he wanted. He had watched Motta win games with defense and like Reinsdorf, who had long admired Red Holzman's New York Knicks, wanted a team that could play both ends of the court.

It took two coaching changes and nearly six seasons, but Krause eventually built a team to complement Jordan's extraordinary talents. The key moves came on a single day in 1987. The Bulls made a deal with Seattle to acquire the draft rights to Scottie Pippen and then selected Horace Grant with their own first-round pick.

A year later the final piece to a championship puzzle arrived in the form of aging 7–1 center Bill Cartwright. Coach Phil Jackson, a player on those Knicks teams that Reinsdorf remembered, built the defense around Jordan, who had become the league's best defensive guard as well as its premier scorer. So it wasn't surprising that the Bulls turned in one of the most dominating playoff performances in history in 1991. Chicago won 15 of 17 playoff games and defeated Magic Johnson's Los Angeles Lakers in the NBA Finals for its first title.

A year later the Bulls won their second straight championship. And then Chicago

ROLL OF HONOR

Conference/Division	Eastern/Central			
First NBA year	1966–67			
Home Arena details	United Center (built 1994, capacity 21,500)			
Former cities/nicknames	None			
NBA Championships	1991, 1992, 1993, 1996, 1997, 1998			

Playing Record	G	W	L	Pct
Regular Season	2541	1378	1163	.542
Playoffs (Series 34–18)	253	147	106	.581

BOB LOVE
A Love Story

That Bob Love, who came from a small Louisiana town with a severe stutter, ever made it in the NBA, much less a record book, is one of the league's great stories of pride and perseverance.

In 1965, Love, a brilliant player at Southern University, wasn't drafted until the fourth round by Cincinnati.

Cut by the Royals, Love ended up in the old Eastern League playing for $50 a game while working part time in a hospital. In 1969, Love joined Chicago.

A year later, Love played all 82 games for the Bulls and led the team in scoring with 21.0 points per game. He went on to lead Chicago in scoring seven straight seasons, never averaging less than 19.1 points a game. Love also made the NBA All-Defensive Second Team three times.

Chicago retired his uniform No. 10 early in the 1993–94 season.

marched back into the Finals for the third consecutive year. Jordan refused to let his team lose. He averaged 41 points in six games against the Suns, scoring 55 in Game 4.

In October 1993, Jordan shocked the basketball world with his retirement, and Chicago was unable to win a fourth straight title. However, when Jordan returned after a season in minor-league baseball, in March 1995, the glamor returned.

After a disappointing loss to the Magic in the 1995 Eastern Conference Finals, the Bulls stormed back to NBA dominance in 1996. Chicago posted an NBA record 72–10 mark in 1995–96, beating Seattle in the NBA Finals. The Bulls fell shy of the 70-win mark in 1996–97 and 1997–98, but both seasons saw the team lay waste to the NBA field come playoff time. The Utah Jazz proved to be worthy adversaries in the 1997 and 1998 NBA Finals, but Chicago won each series in six games. With six of the last eight NBA Championship trophies resting in the Windy City, the Bulls can be sure of their place in history.

Michael Jordan in top form.

Back From The Brink

A little more than a decade after nearly collapsing beneath the weight of bad decisions on and off the court, Cleveland has become one of the NBA's most solid franchises. With a revamped front office, committed ownership and coach Mike Fratello, the Cavaliers consistently rank as an Eastern Conference contender.

For a while, the Cleveland Cavaliers looked like basketball's version of a roller-coaster. The only problem was no one knew for sure whether the Cavaliers would ever pick up enough steam to climb back up after crashing on the way down.

Like most expansion teams, Cleveland started slowly when it got the green light to take off in 1970. Under coach Bill Fitch, the Cavaliers stumbled early and often. They lost the first 15 games in franchise history before slowly gaining control during their first four seasons.

Players such as Bobby "Bingo" Smith, Walt Wesley and Butch Beard, along with top draft picks Austin Carr, Jim Brewer and Campy Russell, helped fuel a steady climb. After 15 wins in their first season, the Cavaliers improved to 40 by 1974–75.

And a year later, thanks to a timely trade, the team started rolling. After a 6–11 start in 1975–76, the Cavaliers traded for aging center Nate Thurmond, a future Hall of Famer. Thurmond's influence helped steady the team, particularly young Jim Chones, and Cleveland began to come together.

The Cavaliers won 43 of their last 65 games to finish 49–33 to charge into the playoffs. Once there, Cleveland dispatched the Washington Bullets in a dramatic seven-game semifinal series. The Cavaliers lost to eventual champion Boston Celtics in the Eastern Conference Finals after Chones was sidelined with a broken foot.

It would be the first in a series of bad breaks for Cleveland. Injuries pushed the team on a downhill course that only gathered greater pace in 1979 when the Cavs franchise was sold to Ted Stepien.

Under Stepien's erratic hand, Cleveland went through seven head coaches (including Bill Musselman twice) and never won more than 28 games from 1980 through 1983. Stepien so mismanaged the team that the NBA executive office actually stepped in and awarded the Cavaliers a "bonus" first-round pick in 1983 in an attempt to salvage the franchise.

By then, however, the Cavaliers had bottomed out. When new owners took over in 1983, the only way to go was up and that's exactly where Cleveland headed once Wayne Embry joined the front office and Lenny Wilkens took over as head coach.

Cleveland traded for center Brad Daugherty on Draft Day in 1986 and never looked back. The Cavaliers added All-Stars Mark Price and Larry Nance via trades and bolstered the bench with draft choices such as John "Hot Rod" Williams and Terrell Brandon.

The combination of off-court leadership and on-court talent made Cleveland one of the most successful teams of the late 1980s. Led by Wilkens' even-handed approach, the Cavaliers became one of the Eastern Conference's most dynamic teams.

The offense, keyed by Daugherty and Price, was smooth and efficient. Wilkens, a former All-Star point guard, developed an unselfish approach that made Cleveland among the most difficult teams in the league to defend. Concentrate too much on Daugherty and Price, one of the NBA's

ROLL OF HONOR

Conference/Division	Eastern/Central			
First NBA year	1970–71			
Home Arena details	Gund Arena (built 1994, capacity 20,562)			
Former cities/nicknames	None			
NBA Championships	None			

Playing Record	G	W	L	Pct
Regular Season	2296	1042	1254	.454
Playoffs (Series 4–13)	77	28	49	.364

finest outside shooters, would bomb away from the outside. The Cavaliers appeared on the verge of a championship during the 1988–89 season when they won 57 games and defeated the Chicago Bulls six times during the regular season.

But the roller coaster ride headed for another set of dips, virtually all of them created by Chicago's Michael Jordan. Jordan's last-second 16-foot jump shot beat Cleveland in the decisive game of the 1989 first-round Playoff series. Jordan's Bulls struck again in 1992 and once more

in 1993, when another last-second Jordan jump shot eliminated the Cavaliers in the Eastern Conference Semifinals.

Mike Fratello took over as Cleveland coach in 1993–94 and he revamped the team from top to bottom. Mark Price was traded away, but young players like point guard Terrell Brandon, swingman Bobby Phills and small forward Chris Mills have stepped to the fore. Small forward Danny Ferry has blossomed into a long-range threat after a lackluster early career.

The Cavaliers were dealt a blow when a

ZYDRUNAS ILGAUSKAS
Questions Answered

It is hard to imagine not expecting big things out of a player 7–3 and 260 pounds. But Cleveland fans didn't know what center Zydrunas Ilgauskas would bring to the table in his first NBA season. The Lithuanian broke his foot in 1996, an injury so severe it would keep him from playing for two years.

Once he took the court for the Cavs, however, all questions were quickly answered. Ilgauskas started his career with a 16-point, 16-rebound performance against the Houston Rockets, and he never looked back. By the end of the 1997–98 season, he ranked as one of the biggest surprises in the game.

Ilgauskas' father, Mecislovas, taught his son the game growing up in Kaunas, Lithuania — the same hometown as Portland star Arvydas Sabonis. Ilgauskas idolized Sabonis, and eventually followed him to the NBA.

"He was my idol, and I felt like he was the best player in the world," says Ilgauskas. "We are friends now, and I am happy to have two Lithuanians playing, from such a small country, in the NBA."

Ilgauskas' first NBA season saw him win the MVP award at the Schick Rookie All-Star Game and finish with averages of 13.9 points and 8.8 rebounds per game. The once unknown commodity has become the cornerstone of the Cavaliers' future.

serious injury forced Daugherty into retirement after the 1995–96 season. Fratello adapted to the change in team chemistry by using a strong defensive system of play that kept the Cavs in playoff contention.

The Cleveland chemistry was altered to a greater degree when trade brought superstar Shawn Kemp from Seattle. While the team lost Brandon in the deal, Kemp added an element of explosiveness long missing from the Cavalier attack. The team also added a cadre of talented rookies—Cedric Henderson, Brevin Knight, Zydrunas Ilgauskas and Derek Anderson—to climb back into the NBA Playoffs and brighten the team's future.

A big deal: Zydrunas Ilgauskas.

DALLAS MAVERICKS

The Long Road Back

For years the Dallas Mavericks were recognized as one of the most successful expansion franchises in league history. Building with young talent, the team charged to the top of the Western Conference before age and disappointing personnel moves led to yet another building program. Dallas has reloaded with new young stars and is ready to return to prominence.

For eight years, Dallas pushed all the right buttons and made all the right calls. From their first season in 1980–81, when Coach Dick Motta, one of the league's master tacticians, poked and prodded a rag-tag expansion roster to 15 victories, the Mavericks defied the gloomiest of expectations.

They improved quickly, winning 43 games in just their fourth season. Three years later, with Motta still at the controls and the roster loaded with talent, Dallas had arrived. The Mavericks took Magic Johnson's Los Angeles Lakers to a seventh game of the Western Conference Finals in 1988. The rise was so rapid and so perfectly executed that Dallas was considered one of the finest organizations in all of professional sports.

Indeed, representatives from Minnesota, Miami, Charlotte and Orlando queried Mavericks' executives prior to joining the league in the NBA's last expansion. How, they all wondered, could a team without a single star player rise to within one game of the NBA Finals in just seven seasons?

Thanks to a tight-knit front office, a solid coaching staff and enlightened player selection, it started with the team's first NBA Draft in 1981, which produced Mark Aguirre, Rolando Blackman and Jay Vincent. Aguirre and Blackman became two of the league's finest scorers, Aguirre the versatile small forward capable of scoring from anywhere on the court and

Drive thru: Michel Finley goes to the paint.

Blackman the true shooting guard with deadly accuracy.

The 1984 Draft produced Sam Perkins, a versatile 6–11 forward who added yet another scorer and inside defense. Detlef Schrempf arrived in the 1985 Draft with towering 7–2 center James Donaldson coming aboard in a trade. The roster appeared virtually complete when the 1986 Draft produced Roy Tarpley, a multi-talented 6–11 forward.

Tarpley, as it turned out, would provide nearly as many negatives as positives. After a memorable seven-year rise, the franchise turned on his misfortunes. A severe knee injury to Tarpley started the Mavericks in a slow spin that eventually landed Dallas right back where it started. Drug problems left Tarpley banished from the league until his reinstatement in the fall of 1994.

Aguirre, who had demanded a trade, went to Detroit for Adrian Dantley. Then the Mavericks traded Schrempf to Indiana for Herb Williams, only to see Schrempf become an All-Star. If that wasn't enough, Donaldson suffered a knee injury. The team fell back into the NBA basement.

The team again retooled itself, adding "The Three J's": shooting guard Jimmy

ROLL OF HONOR

Conference/Division	Western/Midwest			
First NBA year	1980–81			
Home Arena details	Reunion Arena (built 1980, capacity 17,502)			
Former cities/nicknames	None			
NBA Championships	None			
Playing Record	G	W	L	Pct
Regular Season	1394	561	833	.402
Playoffs (Series 4–6)	48	21	27	.438

Jackson, forward Jamal Mashburn and point guard Jason Kidd. By the time the 1996–97 season ended, however, all three star players were gone through separate trades. New general manager Don Nelson, the former Golden State coach, moved all three players in an attempt to rebuild the franchise from the ground up.

The result is a mix of veterans and youngsters fighting to return Dallas to its form of a decade ago. Swingman Michael Finley has blossomed into a star in Big D, becoming a reliable scoring threat with an array of gravity-defying moves. Towering center Shawn Bradley has found a home in the middle of the Mavericks' lineup, while veteran forwards Cedric Ceballos and A.C. Green have brought winning experience to the team. Watch for Nelson to continue wheeling and dealing until the Mavs climb toward the top of the Western Conference.

At 7–6, Shawn Bradley is one foot taller than the man attempting to stop him here, Houston's Charles Barkley.

Hidden Rocky Mountain Highs

The Denver Nuggets' success in the old ABA had started to fizzle by the time they joined the NBA in 1976. Even the franchise's high scoring teams under Coach Doug Moe came during a decade dominated by Magic Johnson's Los Angeles Lakers. That could change soon, however, as Denver has once more started rebuilding with young stars like LaPhonso Ellis, Eric Williams and Bobby Jackson.

For all the flash and dash, the golden years have often come at the wrong time for the Denver Nuggets.

When Coach Larry Brown and high-flying superstar David Thompson were crafting 60-win seasons in the mid 1970s, the Nuggets were one of the most exciting shows in the American Basketball Association. Though the team remained strong after merging with the NBA prior to the 1976–77 season, the next surge didn't come until Doug Moe brought his version of run-and-gun basketball to Denver.

The Nuggets reached the playoffs for nine straight seasons under Moe, but always found one Western Conference team too good for them.

Still, the Nuggets have rarely not shined. As one of the 11 charter members of the ABA in 1967, Denver was recognized as one of that league's best run organizations. Originally called the Rockets, Denver stunned the basketball world in 1969 by signing college undergraduate Spencer Haywood.

Haywood, a star of the U.S. men's gold medal team at the 1968 Olympics Games, played only one season for Denver. But his signing put the franchise on the professional basketball map while also leading to changes in college eligibility rules, many of which are in place today in the NBA.

In 1974, Carl Scheer, an innovative general manager, took over the team and hired Brown as coach. The Nuggets had a new name and a front office full of new faces, but they became instant contenders on the court.

After winning 65 games during the 1974–75 season, Denver loaded up for an ABA title run. Thompson became the first No. 1 NBA draft pick to sign with the ABA. The same season, Denver landed another rookie, Marvin Webster, and veteran Dan Issel. With Thompson and Issel leading the way, Denver went to the ABA championship series before losing to the New Jersey Nets.

It turned out to be the ABA's finale and Denver's only clear shot at a championship. Ensconced in the NBA's reconfigured Midwest Division, the Nuggets continued a franchise tradition of playoff futility. After winning 50 games in 1976–77, Denver ran into the championship-bound Portland Trail Blazers in the Conference Semifinals. A year later, Seattle eliminated the Nuggets in the Western Conference Finals.

And despite continued regular-season success under Moe, the Nuggets never reached the NBA Finals. Still, Denver remained one of the greatest scoring shows in league history. During Moe's nine seasons, Denver led the league in scoring five times and never finished out of the top five.

Players like Thompson, Issel, Alex English, Kiki Vandeweghe, George McGinnis and Lafayette "Fat" Lever fueled a relentless offensive attack that didn't run out of steam until Moe left following the 1989–90 season.

In the 1994 NBA Playoffs, the Nuggets pulled off one of the most dramatic upsets

LAPHONSO ELLIS
The Patrol Man

Growing up on the tough streets of East St. Louis, Ill., LaPhonso Ellis had a dream to grow up and work in a uniform. Not an NBA uniform, but a policeman's uniform. He would watch the endless patrol cars driving through his neighborhood and imagine himself inside.

"I can't remember any of the other kids feeling that way," says Ellis, a 6–8 power forward. "I think that was highly unusual. But those officers were positive role models for me. You couldn't tell me anything negative about police officers."

The discipline that Ellis taught himself in those early years has carried over to his basketball career. Despite major surgery to both kneecaps that caused him to miss the better parts of two seasons in the NBA, Ellis maintained his desire to play for the Nuggets. When he returned in late 1996, it was as if he hadn't missed a beat.

Instead of patrolling the streets of East St. Louis, Ellis patrols the inside of McNichols Arena. Nuggets fans couldn't be happier.

in history, beating the heavily favored Seattle SuperSonics. With Dan Issel at the helm and young players such as center Dikembe Mutombo, point guard Mahmoud Abdul-Rauf, small forward Rodney Rogers and power forward LaPhonso Ellis, the Nuggets looked like a contender in the making.

But injuries put Ellis out for nearly two seasons and Issel stepped down as coach in 1995. The team traded Abdul-Rauf and Rogers for Sarunas Marciulionis and Mark Jackson. Marciulionis missed much of 1996–97 with injuries, Jackson was sent back to Indiana and the Nuggets failed to plug the hole left in the heart of the lineup by Mutombo's free-agent move to Atlanta.

The Nuggets were hit by a bolt of bad luck early in the 1997–98 season when newly acquired forward Eric Williams was lost for the season with a knee injury after just four games. That set the tone for a season that saw Denver total just 11 wins.

The 1998–99 season holds the promise of better days for Rocky Mountain basketball fans. Williams is expected to return at full strength, bringing his 20 points per game average with him. He'll be paired in the frontcourt with Ellis, who has regained his pre-injury form. Point guard Nick Van Exel was acquired from the Lakers to run the point, and rookie center-forward Raef LaFrenz will help round out a strong young lineup that will be trying to paint itself back into the NBA Playoff picture once again.

· ·

After recovering from some serious leg injuries, LaPhonso Ellis is soaring high above the Rocky Mountains once more.

ROLL OF HONOR

Conference/Division	Western/Midwest
First NBA year	1976–77
Home Arena details	McNichols Sports Arena (built 1975, capacity 17,022)
Former cities/nicknames	Denver Rockets (1967–74)
NBA Championships	None

Playing Record	G	W	L	Pct
NBA Regular Season	1804	848	956	.470
Combined NBA/ABA	2548	1261	1277	.495
Playoffs (Series 7–14)	98	39	59	.398
Combined NBA/ABA	160	66	94	.413

Witness for the Defense

They didn't win many friends, but the Detroit Pistons certainly influenced opponents. The Pistons turned to defense in the late 1980s and put on a clinic. With a tough, no-nonsense approach, Detroit became one of the greatest defensive teams in the history of the league. The Pistons won a pair of NBA Championships during a five-year run in which they never finished lower than third in overall team defense. With Joe Dumars as a link between past and present, defense is still the pride of the Pistons.

When Detroit finally won the 1989 NBA title, it ended a 40-year journey that included 21 head coaches, a move and a 15-year stretch without one winning season. Even after the team moved from Fort Wayne, Indiana, to Detroit for the 1957–58 season, 13 straight losing seasons followed.

The franchise started out as the after-hours avocation of Fort Wayne manufacturer Fred Zollner, who owned a factory that made automobile pistons. Zollner

first organized the team in 1937, more than a decade before the NBA started. Throughout the mid 1940s, Zollner's Pistons were one of the top teams in the National Basketball League, winning consecutive titles in 1944–45.

But all that changed when the NBL survivors, including Detroit, joined the NBA. The Pistons immediately established what would become a long-running reputation as everyone's favorite opponent despite some solid, early talent. Not even players such as George Yardley, Max Zaslofsky, Larry Foust and Andy Phillip could prevent the Pistons from general mediocrity during their first decade in the league.

Under coach Charlie Eckman, a former referee, Fort Wayne reached the NBA Finals in 1955 and 1956, but following the move to Detroit in 1957, a .500 playing record was beyond the Pistons.

The first of two major upturns followed with the arrival of 6–11 giant Bob Lanier, Detroit's No. 1 pick in the 1970 Draft. Three years later, the Pistons finished 52–30, their best record to that point, but fell to the Chicago Bulls in the Western Conference Semifinals.

By 1979 Lanier and long-time backcourt star Dave Bing had been traded and Detroit

Detroit's Joe Dumars is the ultimate class act.

were again one of the league's worst teams. But out of the ashes of a 16–66 1979–80 season rose a Detroit team that came to

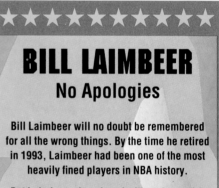

BILL LAIMBEER
No Apologies

Bill Laimbeer will no doubt be remembered for all the wrong things. By the time he retired in 1993, Laimbeer had been one of the most heavily fined players in NBA history.

But Laimbeer also played with an iron spirit that carried him through a 14-year career. Upon leaving Notre Dame Laimbeer spent one season in Europe before signing with Cleveland in 1981. Two years later he landed in Detroit and became an instant contributor.

During Laimbeer's first nine years with the Pistons, he was the team's starting center in 736 of 738 regular season games and never missed a playoff game. He also became a key component in the team's back-to-back championships in 1989 and 1990.

Laimbeer, who had his No. 40 jersey retired by the Pistons in 1995, is Detroit's all-time leader in rebounds and games played, missing just nine games in his 13 full seasons.

Hill the Thrill: Grant Hill is one of the game's most popular players.

Lakers and Magic Johnson 4–0 in the best-of-7 NBA Finals, then adding a second title in 1990 by downing Portland, 4–1.

Daly left after the 1992 season, and the only member of Detroit's championship nucleus to remain in the Motor City is Dumars. The highly respected shooting guard is now the elder statesman on a young team with a bright future.

The Pistons' road back to the NBA Finals took a detour in 1997–98. Former Miami Heat coach Alvin Gentry took over the team in midseason, but he could not guide the team to the playoffs. With superstar forward Grant Hill leading the way, Detroit could get back on track in a hurry. Hill is among the league's most versatile players, leading the league in triple-doubles and improving the play of his teammates along the way. Slashing swingman Jerry Stackhouse and center Brian Williams join Hill and Dumars in providing scoring punch, while cat-quick Lindsey Hunter hounds opposing point guards all over the court. With some minor repairs, Motown could be motoring back toward the winners' circle.

dominate the late 1980s.

The Pistons used their No. 1 pick in the 1981 Draft to select Thomas, who became one of the most accomplished point guards in NBA history. Joe Dumars arrived in the 1985 Draft followed by Dennis Rodman and John Salley in 1986. Trades produced Bill Laimbeer, Vinnie Johnson, Mark Aguirre and James Edwards.

Coach Chuck Daly molded the team into a bruising defensive squad built on strength and toughness. They pushed, shoved, scratched and clawed their way to consecutive championships, winning their first in 1989 by sweeping the Los Angeles

ROLL OF HONOR

Conference/Division	Eastern/Central			
First NBA year	1948–49			
Home Arena details	The Palace of Auburn Hills (built 1988, capacity 21,454)			
Former cities/nicknames	Fort Wayne Pistons (1948–57)			
NBA Championships	1989, 1990			

Playing Record	G	W	L	Pct
Regular Season	3940	1874	2066	.476
Playoffs (Series 23–27)	224	113	111	.504

Back to the Drawing Board

It wasn't long ago that the Warriors boasted star players like Mitch Richmond, Tim Hardaway, Chris Mullin, Latrell Sprewell and Joe Smith in the team's lineup. But all have moved on to other teams, leaving coach P.J. Carlesimo the task of rebuilding a once-great franchise. With Jim Jackson, Donyell Marshall and Muggsy Bogues donning the lightning bolt logo, that goal is within reach.

Another rise has led to another brief fall and the Warriors once again are headed back to the future.

The Philadelphia Warriors began play in 1946 as charter members of the 11-team Basketball Association of America. Under the leadership of local basketball legend Eddie Gottlieb and with players such as Joe Fulks, Howie Dallmar and George Senesky, the Warriors won the first ever BAA title. Nine years later, the Warriors captured another championship, this time in the reconfigured NBA. With Senesky as coach, legendary players such as Paul Arizin and Neil Johnston led Philadelphia to a 45–27 regular-season record and an easy rout of the Fort Wayne Pistons in the 1956 Finals.

In 1959, Gottlieb convinced his fellow owners to allow Philadelphia a non-traditional "territorial" draft pick. In that era, each NBA team was allowed to choose one college player from the geographic area of the team's dominant fan base. Gottlieb's coup was predicated on the fact that Wilt Chamberlain had played high school ball in Philadelphia, although he was attending college at the University of Kansas.

Wilt 'The Stilt' became the greatest scoring machine in NBA history. He stood 7–1, weighed 275 pounds, and was the most dominant individual player the league had ever known. He averaged a phenomenal 50.4 points a game during the 1961–62 season for Philadelphia.

But not even Chamberlain could carry an entire franchise by himself. With attendance lagging, Gottlieb sold the team to a San Francisco group that moved the Warriors west for the 1962–63 season.

Two years later, the Warriors were once again building for a championship run. Nate Thurmond, who would become another of the great NBA centers, arrived. San Francisco then dealt Chamberlain to the new Philadelphia franchise. Thurmond was soon surrounded by players such as Rick Barry, Jeff Mullins, Al Attles and Clyde Lee. And in 1967, the Warriors found themselves back in the NBA Finals, this time against Chamberlain's Philadelphia 76ers, who took the championship 4–2.

It took another 10-year cycle before the Warriors reached the Finals again. With Attles as coach and Barry leading the team in scoring, Golden State, which moved to Oakland from San Francisco in 1971, swept the Washington Bullets 4–0 for the 1975 NBA Championship.

But another downturn began during the next decade. It wasn't until yet another new ownership group hired Don Nelson that the franchise took off again. He brought the Warriors back to life. With talented players such as Chris Mullin, Sarunas Marciulionis, Billy Owens, and Tim Hardaway, the team won 55 games in 1991–92.

Three years later, fresh off a Draft-day trade that produced a potential superstar in

Chris Webber, the Warriors appeared primed for another run at the title. Latrell Sprewell, a gifted and versatile guard, had been added to an arsenal built around Mullin and Hardaway to make the Warriors virtually impossible to stop.

Mullin, one of the NBA's greatest shoot-

ABOVE: The No. 1 pick of the 1995 NBA Draft, Joe Smith, left Golden State after three seasons.

ers, opened to the floor Sprewell and Hardaway. And for the 1994–95 season, Golden State added former Miami center Rony Seikaly. With Webber and Seikaly up front, the Warriors appeared to have plugged the team's only remaining holes.

But all the hope dissolved amid injuries to Hardaway and Mullin and a conflict between Nelson and Webber. Golden State traded Webber to Washington for Tom Gugliotta and draft picks. Everything became even more clouded as the season dragged on. More injuries to Mullin, Seikaly and Hardaway made things worse. Gugliotta was soon sent to Minnesota for forward Donyell Marshall and Nelson resigned.

Hardaway, Mullin and Sprewell have all moved on, and coach P.J. Carlesimo is building a new core of stars in the Bay Area. Swingman Jimmy Jackson and forward Clarence Weatherspoon were acquired from

ROLL OF HONOR

Conference/Division	Western/Pacific			
First NBA year	1946–47			
Home Arena details	Coliseum Arena (built 1966, capacity 19,200)			
Former cities/nicknames	Philadelphia Warriors (1946–62), San Francisco Warriors (1962–71)			
NBA Championships	1947, 1956, 1975			
Playing Record	G	W	L	Pct
Regular Season	3964	1908	2056	.481
Playoffs (Series 22–24)	214	99	115	.463

Philadelphia, and both adjusted well to the West Coast. Forward Donyell Marshall earned a bigger role in the Warriors' plans by showcasing the all-around skills that made him a recent NBA Draft lottery pick,

while second-year center Errick Dampier took great strides toward plugging the mammoth hole Golden State has had in the middle for several seasons. With more time to jell as a team, Carlesimo's Warriors hope to tower over the NBA landscape like the nearby Golden Gate Bridge.

Two for 22: Golden State's Jim Jackson will not be denied.

MUGGSY BOGUES
Little Big Man By the Bay

Tyrone "Muggsy" Bogues has never thought of himself as being small. Although standing just 5–3 and playing a game dominated by giants, he hardly notices.

"They're just taller than me," says Bogues.

Even after a solid college career at Wake Forest, few thought Bogues could be a success in the NBA. But Washington used the No. 12 pick in the 1987 NBA Draft to select him, where he became a teammate of the NBA's tallest player, 7–7 Manute Bol.

A year later, Charlotte selected Bogues in the 1988 expansion draft. Despite his size, he became a fixture in the Hornets' starting lineup and a fan favorite in Charlotte.

Bogues left Charlotte for Golden State at the start of the 1997–98 season, and he became a key contributor as the Warriors' floor general. With his incredible quickness and a sixth sense for the ball, Bogues has overcome any problems his size might create.

The Dream Is Real

Houston used an enormous front line to reach the 1986 NBA Finals. But after Larry Bird's Boston Celtics ended those title dreams, the Rockets took nearly a decade to find a way back. With former star Rudy Tomjanovich coaching and superstar Hakeem "The Dream" Olajuwon doing just about everything else, Houston knocked off New York in a thrilling Game 7 to claim its first championship in 1994 and swept Orlando to repeat in 1995.

Until their dramatic victory in the 1994 NBA Finals, one question had dogged Houston for nearly 20 years. How could a team have had players such as Elvin Hayes, Moses Malone, Ralph Sampson and Hakeem Olajuwon, all as rookies, and reach the early 1990s without a single NBA Championship?

The San Diego Rockets joined the NBA in 1967. As with most expansion teams, the first season was a long one. The result, however, was that San Diego had the No. 1 pick in the 1968 Draft and it produced the multi-talented Hayes. Though the 6–9 forward led the league in scoring in his rookie season, teams then double- and triple-teamed him, making other Rockets beat them. It rarely happened. By 1971, the Rockets were still a sub-.500 team and attendance had fallen off in San Diego.

Rudy Tomjanovich gets his point across.

A move to Houston followed, but so too did the losses. A feud between coach Tex Winter and Hayes led to the player being traded in 1972. Despite the presence of young stars like Calvin Murphy and Rudy Tomjanovich, the Rockets needed four years to recover from the Hayes trade. It wasn't until rookie John Lucas and Moses Malone arrived in 1976 that the franchise moved over the .500 mark for the first time. Malone helped lead Houston to 49 victories and the Central Division title.

But once again, the future wasn't nearly as bright as expected. This time a near tragedy played a part. On December 9, 1977, in a game at Los Angeles, a fight broke out between the Rockets and Lakers. Tomjanovich, trying to be a peacemaker, ran into a punch thrown by Kermit Washington and ended up in critical condition with terrible facial injuries. Though he eventually recovered, the team slumped to 54 losses.

In 1981, with Malone and Murphy leading the way, the Rockets upset Magic Johnson's Los Angeles Lakers in the First Round of the Playoffs. Then they dispatched Midwest Division champion San Antonio and rival Kansas City before losing to Boston in the Finals. Once more success was fleeting. Within two years, the Rockets were the worst team in basketball. Malone signed with Philadelphia and Houston found itself looking for another great, young center.

Thanks to the NBA Draft, the Rockets found two of them. They drafted 7–4 Ralph

R O L L   O F   H O N O R

Conference/Division	Western/Midwest			
First NBA year	1967–68			
Home Arena details	The Summit (built 1975, capacity 16,279)			
Former cities/nicknames	San Diego Rockets (1967–71)			
NBA Championships	1994, 1995			

Playing Record	G	W	L	Pct
Regular Season	2542	1266	1276	.498
Playoffs (Series 22–18)	195	99	96	.508

Sampson with the No. 1 pick in 1983 and then Hakeem Olajuwon with the first pick in 1984. That duo combined with young Rodney McCray to create one of the most imposing frontlines of that era. Houston reached the 1986 NBA Finals but lost valiantly to the Boston Celtics in six games.

Although Sampson was traded in 1989, the Rockets remained dangerous thanks to Olajuwon, but the team didn't come together completely until Tomjanovich took over as head coach in 1992. With Olajuwon, Otis Thorpe, Vernon Maxwell and Kenny Smith leading the way, Houston reached the 1993 Western Conference Semifinals.

It was only the beginning. A year later, the same nucleus carried Houston to victory over Patrick Ewing's New York Knicks in Game 7 of the 1994 Finals, giving Houston its first NBA Championship.

In 1995, the defending champion Rockets became the first-ever sixth seed to win the title, sweeping Orlando in the Finals, and the

fourth consecutive repeat NBA Champion. Houston also set a record by winning seven straight playoff games on the road.

The 1995–96 season saw an unprecedented number of injuries hit Houston. Every important member of the team was sidelined, with major injuries to shooting guard Clyde Drexler and forward Mario Elie. The Rockets made do during the regular season with a makeshift lineup, but they couldn't put together an extended playoff run.

Houston traded for superstar forward Charles Barkley in 1996, adding another dimension to an already powerful nucleus. While the Rockets' playoff streak was extended to six in the 1997–98 season, injuries and age conspired to keep the team from returning to the NBA Finals. Drexler retired after the season, and Olajuwon and Barkley will have to come back strong from nagging injuries to return the Rockets to the top of the Western Conference.

Hakeem "The Dream" Olajuwon can be a nightmare for opponents.

★★★★★★★★★★★★

RUDY TOMJANOVICH

Blast from the Past

Midway through the 1991–92 season the Houston Rockets were out of experiments. They had tried virtually everything in search of an elusive NBA Championship.

With the team stuck with a 26–26 record, the franchise finally decided to try one of its own. Rudy Tomjanovich had been a member of the organization since 1970 when he joined the Rockets out of the University of Michigan.

By the time Houston named Tomjanovich interim head coach, he had been involved in the franchise's only two division championships and ranked third on the team's all-time scoring list. The team finished 16–14 under Tomjanovich.

The Rockets had found the man they needed. Houston finished 55–27 in 1992–93 to win the Midwest Division and Tomjanovich was named IBM NBA Coach of the Year. He topped that feat by coaching Houston to back-to-back NBA Championships in 1994 and 1995.

Taking Wing with Bird

The Indiana Pacers have one of the more storied histories in all of basketball, but virtually all of it occurred before the team joined the NBA in 1976. As a charter member of the American Basketball Association, Indiana had some of the most dominant teams in that league's brief history. New coach Larry Bird, an NBA legend and native Hoosier, will try to restore the Pacers to greatness.

Despite being situated in a state known for its wildly devoted basketball fans, the Indiana Pacers have spent much of their NBA existence trying to develop a following.

High school basketball has its roots in the small towns of Indiana, while Indiana University has one of the most visible programs in the country. So when the Pacers entered the old ABA as a charter member in 1967, they had much to prove.

They never blinked.

With early stars like Mel Daniels, Roger Brown and Freddie Lewis, Indiana won 59 games and the ABA championship in 1970. One year later, the Pacers stepped on the toes of neighboring Indiana University by signing undergraduate George McGinnis, a brilliant young forward.

McGinnis paid off immediately. He led the Pacers to consecutive ABA titles. Under the leadership of coach Bobby "Slick" Leonard, the Pacers were a hit on and off the court. Indiana was one of the four surviving ABA franchises to join the NBA in 1976.

But that signaled the end of an era for the Pacers. Leonard was faced with a massive rebuilding job after McGinnis signed with the Philadelphia 76ers in 1975 and age caught up with the rest of the ABA cast.

Selfless Don Buse and high-scoring Billy Knight were the Pacers' early NBA stars, but the franchise never quite got rolling. The team's first NBA Playoff series didn't come

ROLL OF HONOR

Conference/Division	Eastern/Central			
First NBA year	1976-77 (ABA 1967-76)			
Home Arena details	Market Square Arena (built 1974, capacity 16,530)			
Former cities/nicknames	None			
NBA Championships	None (ABA — 1970, 1972, 1973)			

Playing Record	G	W	L	Pct
NBA Regular Season	1804	834	970	.462
Combined NBA/ABA	2548	1261	1287	.495
Playoffs (Series 6–9)	75	36	39	.480
Combined NBA/ABA	194	105	89	.538

After a legendary playing career in Boston, can Larry Bird lead Indiana to an NBA Championship?

out in 1994. After a franchise-best 47 regular season wins, Indiana got to the Eastern Conference Finals, but the Pacers lost a dramatic Game 7 in New York. In 1995 they lost again in the seventh game of the Eastern Conference Finals, this time to Orlando.

1996–97 was a disappointing season for Indiana, but the future became brighter with the hiring of the legendary Larry Bird, an Indiana native, as coach. The former Celtics and college basketball superstar was named 1997–98 IBM NBA Coach of the Year, and the Pacers served notice that they were ready to challenge the Bulls' dominance. Indeed, the Pacers took the Bulls to the final moments of a seventh game in the Eastern Conference finals before losing. But with Bird in charge, look for Indiana to set the NBA pace for years to come.

Reggie Miller (right) is not afraid to battle with the biggest of bodies.

★★★★★★★★★★

RIK SMITS
Indiana's Gentle Giant

Long before Rik Smits crossed the Atlantic Ocean on his way to an NBA career, he could be found on basketball courts in Eindhoven, Holland. Though blessed with unusual size (he stands 7–4) and excellent coordination, Smits hadn't had the typical early training of American players by the time he left Holland for the relative obscurity of tiny Marist College in New York.

But the Indiana Pacers took notice and were so impressed they made him the second overall pick in the 1988 NBA Draft. Smits has occupied the middle of the Indiana offense and defense ever since. His soft shooting touch has helped open Indiana's outside game for teammates like Reggie Miller.

Smits scored a career-best 17.9 points per game while shooting 52.6 percent from the floor in 1995. Severe foot injuries kept him off the court for much of the 1996–97 season, but a return to form—with guidance from new coach Larry Bird—is in the cards for the big center.

until 1981, a 3-game sweep by the 76ers, led by ex-Pacer McGinnins, and the Pacers didn't *win* a playoff game until 1987. Along the way there were seven coaches and a four-year period in the early 1980s when Indiana averaged 58 losses per season.

But the Pacers have not been without some individual gems even during the most trying times. Players such as Steve Stipanovich, Detlef Schrempf, Clark Kellogg, Wayman Tisdale, Herb Williams, Chuck Person, and others too, have passed through Indiana's franchise.

The team, coached by the legendary Jack Ramsay, finished 41–41 and reached the Playoffs in 1987. Indiana not only earned its first playoff victory, but it appeared to have

finally turned itself around.

But Kellogg, who had suffered a severe knee injury four games into the 1986–87 season, never returned. A year later, Stipanovich, a 7-foot center who had developed into a solid player, suffered a career-ending injury. Suddenly, the Pacers were losing games in bunches once more.

Another injection of young talent helped bring Indiana back into the playoff picture. Reggie Miller, one of the league's finest shooters, and 7–4 center Rik Smits helped the Pacers into the playoffs six straight seasons through the 1994–95 campaign.

With coach Larry Brown in control of the team and Derrick McKey arriving in a trade for Schrempf, the Pacers finally broke

Still Striving For Success

No franchise has tried harder or struggled longer than the Los Angeles Clippers. Originally known as the Buffalo Braves, the team moved to San Diego and then Los Angeles. Once there the franchise was overshadowed by the brilliant Los Angeles Lakers teams led by Magic Johnson. For 12 straight seasons in the late 1970s and 1980s, the Clippers failed to register a winning season. Though the Clippers rose briefly in the early 1990s, the struggle hasn't ended yet.

When the Los Angeles Clippers moved from San Diego in 1984, some worried about the franchise having an identity crisis. After all, one of the league's most successful franchises, the Lakers, had long been a resident of Los Angeles.

Indeed, no team has suffered as much or as long as the Clippers in what seems to be a unending quest for respectability. Since they entered the league as the Buffalo Braves in 1970, the Los Angeles Clippers have won more than half their games just five times. They went 15 straight seasons without a playoff appearance from 1976 through 1991. And to make matters worse, the Clippers had nine different coaches in 11 years, the latest being Bill Fitch who took over in 1994.

The franchise started its long climb as one of three expansion teams, along with Cleveland and Portland, added for the 1970–71 season. Thanks to wise drafting and the addition of Coach Jack Ramsay, Buffalo had a flashy young lineup loaded with potential by its fourth NBA season.

High-scoring center/forward Bob McAdoo — who led the league with more than 30 points per game — along with Jack Marin, Ernie DiGregorio, Garfield Heard, Randy Smith and Jim McMillan, led the Braves into the playoffs. In 1974,

Lamond Murray rises above the nets.

Buffalo was the NBA's best offensive team.

The team won 49 games the following season and then 46, each followed by strong, yet limited playoff performances. But the future disintegrated just as it appeared to be taking shape. Ramsay resigned to take over in Portland. McMillan and DiGregorio were traded and, in a move that disillusioned Buffalo fans, McAdoo was dealt along with future United States Congressman Tom McMillen to the New

ROLL OF HONOR

Conference/Division	Western/Pacific			
First NBA year	1970–71			
Home Arena details	LA Memorial Sports Arena (built 1959, capacity 16,005)			
Former cities/nicknames	Buffalo Braves (1970–78), San Diego Clippers (1978–84)			
NBA Championships	None			

Playing Record	G	W	L	Pct
Regular Season	2296	831	1465	.362
Playoffs (Series 1–6)	35	13	22	.371

York Knicks for cash and journeyman center John Gianelli. The moves, coupled with disappointing results on the court, led to poor attendance and the franchise's eventual relocation to San Diego. With Gene Shue now in as coach, the Clippers posted a 43–39 record in 1978–79, their last winning mark for more than a decade.

Once again, a disastrous off-season trade undermined the franchise. This time Kermit Washington, Kevin Kunnert, a first-round pick and cash were shipped to Portland for the remarkable, but often injured Bill Walton. Unfortunately, the trade only made things more difficult. Walton, a wondrously talented center, played just 14 games over the next three seasons and the Clippers went into a tailspin.

Although poor seasons translated into great draft positions, the Clippers failed to benefit. From 1987 through 1989, the team used six first-round picks on Reggie Williams, Joe Wolf, Ken Norman, Danny Manning, Hersey Hawkins and Danny Ferry, none of whom were with the team when the 1994–95 season started.

The Clippers finally found a measure of success when Larry Brown became coach during the 1991–92 season. They finished 23–12 over their last 35 games and made the playoffs for the first time since 1976. The team made a return trip in 1993 before problems surfaced again.

Brown left for Indiana, and Norman, Ron Harper and Dominique Wilkins, who had been traded for Manning, left as free agents. A revamped Clippers squad—led by steady power forward Loy Vaught, forward Rodney Rogers and young center Lorenzen Wright—broke back into the NBA Playoffs after the 1996–97 regular season.

The 1997 NBA Draft brought forward Maurice Taylor, who became an All-Rookie Team selection, and center Michael Olowokandi was added with the No. 1 pick in the 1998 NBA Draft. Olowokandi — a Nigerian by way of England — could be the NBA's next dominant center, which is why the Clippers are feeling chipper when they think of the future.

The Clippers' Loy Vaught (35, right) readies to drive to the hoop.

LOY VAUGHT
Coming on Strong

Loy Vaught had played in the shadows so long that not even he knew what would happen when he emerged.

At the University of Michigan, Vaught played with stars like Glen Rice, Gary Grant and Rumeal Robinson. Since Vaught joined the Clippers as a first-round pick in the 1990 NBA Draft, Danny Manning, Ron Harper, Dominique Wilkins and others have all passed through Los Angeles.

But when the 1994–95 season opened, so too did Vaught's opportunity. He was the only regular that had been with the Clippers more than three seasons, during which time Vaught had developed into a solid power forward.

In 1993–94, Vaught improved his field goal percentage for the fourth consecutive season to an impressive .537. He added career bests in rebounds, steals, assists points. And in 1994–95, Vaught stepped up as the Clippers' leading scorer and rebounder at 17.5 ppg and 9.7 rpg.

"I've always been, and I prefer to be, a complementary player," says Vaught. "So this is a little different."

So far, however, the Clippers aren't complaining. For a team in need of a foundation, a 6-9, 240-pound forward with Vaught's work ethic is a nice place to start.

The West's Winningest Team

The names are some of the most famous in all of professional basketball. Players like George Mikan, Jerry West, Elgin Baylor, Wilt Chamberlain, Kareem Abdul-Jabbar and Magic Johnson all played on Lakers teams that won NBA Championships. Now the Lakers have added another big name—Shaquille O'Neal. Forget "Showtime," the Lakers are now "Shaqtime."

The Lakers began life in Minneapolis. They have won 11 Championships, 24 conference titles and own the second best winning percentage in NBA history, .608 entering the 1997–98 season. Only the Celtics, which had won 61.4 percent of their regular season games after the 1996–97 season, have won more often.

The team was named after the state of Minnesota's claim as the "Land of 10,000 Lakes." It also earned its first championships there, with George Mikan manning the middle. Mikan, who was basketball's first dominant big man, stood 6–10 and won three straight scoring titles after the Lakers became part of the NBA in 1948.

Eddie Jones finds the fast track to the basket.

Mikan played on seven championship teams in his first eight professional season, the first two for Chicago in the old National Basketball League. When that team disbanded, Mikan landed with the Minneapolis franchise in the NBA and helped that team to five titles in six years. Mikan's supporting cast included Slater Martin, Vern Mikkelsen, Jim Pollard and 1952 U.S. Olympic team hero Clyde Lovellette. When Mikan retired after the 1953–54 season—the Lakers' last championship in the Midwest—the team needed a new star. They found one in 1958 when University of Seattle star Elgin Baylor was signed. Minneapolis reached the NBA Finals in 1959, but quickly fell to Boston. But a year later the team moved to Los Angeles.

Despite a talented roster that included Baylor and Jerry West, the Lakers kept running into Boston. From 1961 through 1970, Los Angeles won seven Western Division championships. But they lost all seven Finals, six to the Celtics.

Los Angeles' NBA frustrations ended briefly in 1971–72, when an aging Wilt Chamberlain joined the team. In the greatest single season at that point in NBA history, the Lakers set records with a 33-game winning streak and a 69–13 record.

Though the Lakers reached the Finals the following season, they didn't win another Championship until Johnson arrived in 1979. The team won a coin flip with the Chicago Bulls for the No. 1 pick in the 1979 Draft and chose Johnson.

The 6–9 guard teamed with another legendary big man, Kareem Abdul-Jabbar, and quickly helped the Lakers become the dom-

★ ★ ★ ★ ★ ★ ★ ★ ★ ★

JERRY WEST
All-Around Brilliance

Until Michael Jordan teamed with Magic Johnson on the Dream Team, the world had never seen a better backcourt than that of Jerry West and Oscar Robertson during the 1960 Rome Olympics.

In fact, until Jordan, West and Robertson were considered the two greatest shooting guards to ever play the game. Shorter at 6–2 and a more pure shooter and defender, West and the 6–5 Robertson went head-to-head through their entire NBA careers.

Despite leading the Lakers into the NBA Finals nine times, West's only championship came in 1972. But he knew how to win, as evidenced by a career that remains among the most successful in history.

West led the Lakers to the 1977 Pacific Division title in his first year as the team's head coach. Four years later, West moved to the front office and carefully constructed a Lakers team that would dominate the 1980s.

inant team of the 1980s. The head-to-head matchups with Boston continued, but this time the Lakers came out on top often—winning twice in three NBA Finals meetings.

Los Angeles, with supporting players such as Jamaal Wilkes, James Worthy, Byron Scott, Norm Nixon and Michael Cooper, won five championships in Johnson's first nine seasons. Johnson and Bird, like Chamberlain and Russell before them, identified an entire decade. Indeed their battles might have been the greatest in league history given their respective skills.

As with Boston, however, those days have given way to another rebuilding process. And that process, at least for the Lakers, appeared to pick up steam during the 1994–95 season. With veteran coach Del

ROLL OF HONOR

Conference/Division	Western/Pacific			
First NBA year	1948–49			
Home Arena details	The Great Western Forum (built 1967, capacity 17,505)			
Former cities/nicknames	Minneapolis Lakers (1948–60)			
NBA Championships	1949, 1950, 1952, 1953, 1954, 1972, 1980, 1982, 1985, 1987, 1988			

Playing Record	G	W	L	Pct
Regular Season	3941	2409	1532	.611
Playoffs (Series 76–35)	529	312	217	.590

Harris taking over the coaching duties, young players Nick Van Exel and Eddie Jones combined with veterans Cedric Ceballos, Vlade Divac and Elden Campbell to give the franchise new life.

Late in the 1995–96 season, the NBA was treated to a comeback from Johnson, who still had the old magic. Playing both power forward and point guard, Magic tried to teach his younger teammates about winning in the playoffs. Yet even Johnson's return failed to rally the Lakers past the Rockets in the first round of the playoffs.

The 1996–97 season saw Magic retire again, but a new attraction opened in Tinseltown. Shaquille O'Neal brought his dominant inside game—and budding music and movie career—to Los Angeles, giving the Lakers a dominant center for the first time since Abdul-Jabbar's retirement.

Joining Shaq at the top of the Hollywood marquee is guard Kobe Bryant, just two years removed from high school and already an NBA All-Star. The spectacular supporting cast includes high-flying swingman Eddie Jones and former Rockets forward Robert Horry. Don't be surprised to see this exciting young group of stars leading the Lakers to a new championship era.

Kobe Bryant soars over Greg Ostertag to drop in two more points for the Los Angeles Lakers.

Not
Standing Pat

With a solid plan and front office patience, the Heat took just four seasons to reach the playoffs after joining the NBA as an expansion franchise in 1988. Miami improved each of its first four seasons in the league before injuries slowed its progress. Now the Heat has gone back to the drawing board in hopes of reclaiming its future. Coach Pat Riley and center Alonzo Mourning are trying to turn the Heat around.

Few NBA expansion franchises have come together with the class and conviction of Miami. While former NBA great Billy Cunningham dreamed of a team in Miami, a city that until 1988 had only one professional sports team in football's Dolphins, critics wondered whether locals would gather regularly to watch basketball, particularly the NBA brand.

But Cunningham persevered. He lined up investors such as Zev Bufman, a highly suc-

He's On Fire: Alonzo Mourning.

cessful Broadway producer, Ted Arison, owner of the Carnival Cruise Lines, and long-time NBA executive Lewis Schaffel.

With indisputable credentials, Cunningham's group was awarded an NBA franchise in April, 1987. The team took the nickname the "Heat" and Cunningham and Schaffel went to work on building a roster. Miami played its first game 18 months later, joining Charlotte for the 1988–89 season.

Two of Miami's early building blocks were on the team opening night. Center Rony Seikaly, a first-round pick in the 1988 draft, and Grant Long, a hard-working forward, joined a group of veterans that included Jon Sunvold and Rory Sparrow. Not surprisingly, the Heat stumbled badly losing its first 17 NBA games and finishing just 15–67. Rookies Glen Rice and Sherman Douglas arrived for the 1989–90 season, but the young Heat continued to stumble and fall, this time to 66 losses.

By the third season, however, Miami had quietly assembled a nucleus of young talent. Though they were still learning on the job—Miami finished 24–58—the future was slowly coming into focus. That's when Cunningham turned to long-time friend and former teammate Kevin Loughery to assume the coaching reins.

Loughery's first team finished 38–44 and became the first of the four newest expansion teams to reach the playoffs. Rookie point guard Steve Smith proved to be even better than advertised while Rice had developed into one of the NBA's finest long-range shooters. Seikaly improved to 16.8 points and 11.8 rebounds a game and Miami appeared to be progressing ahead of even its own long-term schedule.

A rash of injuries jolted the Heat during the 1992–93 season. Despite adding flashy rookie Harold Miner and trading for forward John Salley, Miami slipped to 36–46 and failed to reach the playoffs. A season which started with high expectations faded fast as injuries to Salley, Seikaly, Smith and Willie Burton took their toll. Salley missed 31 games, Smith 34, Burton 56 and Seikaly 10. Only two players on the roster appeared in more than 73 of the Heat's 82 games.

Still, there remained plenty of reason for optimism as Miami returned to the Playoffs in 1994. Within months, however, a cloud had parked over Miami: Brian Shaw left via free agency; Smith, Long, Burton and Seikaly were traded away; Loughery was replaced by his assistant, Alvin Gentry, midway through the season, and the ownership, controlled by Cunningham and Schaffel, sold its interest and moved on.

For Miami, the task of rebuilding was given to former NBA player and coach Dave

ROLL OF HONOR

Conference/Division	Eastern/Atlantic			
First NBA year	1988–89			
Home Arena details	Miami Arena (built 1988, capacity 15,200)			
Former cities/nicknames	None			
NBA Championships	None			

	G	W	L	Pct
Playing Record				
Regular Season	820	363	457	.443
Playoffs (Series 2–5)	33	12	21	.364

Wohl, as the team's general manager. The on-court future was placed in the capable hands of Pat Riley. The former Lakers and Knicks coach wasted no time making changes to the Heat. Center Alonzo Mourning and point guard Tim Hardaway were added during the 1995–96 season, and Miami learned to play Riley's stifling brand of defense. Mourning flourished, becoming the team's leader.

The following two seasons saw the Heat win back-to-back Atlantic Division titles for the first time in franchise history despite a rash of injuries each campaign. Hardaway regained his status as one of the league's most potent point guards, capable of destroying defenses with passes, long-range bombs or his trademark crossover dribble move. Outside snipers such as Voshon Lenard and Dan Majerle helped balance the inside threat of Mourning and forward Jamal Mashburn. With Riley's patented defense in place, the Heat hope to erase the memory of a first-round playoff loss to the Knicks with another playoff march in 1999.

• •

Pat Riley: One of the NBA's greatest coaches.

Rebuilding for the Future

Although the Milwaukee Bucks reached the playoffs for 12 straight seasons from 1980 through 1991, they were never quite good enough to reach the NBA Finals. Now the franchise is working on a new look. The roster is younger, the defense better and the future brighter. Glenn Robinson, Ray Allen and Terrell Brandon are trying to recapture Milwaukee's past glory.

Few will ever forget the one stroke of luck that turned an expansion franchise into an NBA champion in just three seasons. Basketball history turned on the flip of a single coin in 1969. The Bucks had entered the NBA prior to the 1968–69 season and proceeded to lose 55 games. There were only two divisions in those days, and Phoenix, another expansion team that season, lost 66 games to finish last in the West. Since Milwaukee occupied the bottom spot in the East, a coin flip determined which team would have the No. 1 draft pick in 1969.

No game for either team had been as big as the coin flip. The winner would get 7–2 center Kareem Abdul-Jabbar (then known as Lew Alcindor), at the time the most accomplished center to leave the college ranks since Bill Russell and Wilt Chamberlain. And he didn't disappoint.

Phoenix called heads, the coin came up tails and Milwaukee became an instant contender. Abdul-Jabbar averaged 28.8 points and 14.5 rebounds as a rookie and the Bucks

reversed their 1969 record to win 55 games.

Milwaukee then added aging superstar Oscar Robertson prior to the 1970–71 season to run the offense and take pressure off the young Abdul-Jabbar. The Bucks dominated the league, winning 66 games and cruising through the playoffs. They pounded Baltimore in the Finals, winning four straight games by an average of more than 12 points.

Though Abdul-Jabbar led the Bucks to an average of 61 victories over the next three seasons, Milwaukee reached the NBA Finals only once more, in 1974, losing in seven games to Boston. Injuries plagued Abdul-Jabbar's final season in Milwaukee and the team dipped to 38–44. The Bucks decided to trade Abdul-Jabbar to the Los Angeles Lakers prior to the 1975–76 season. The deal, with journeyman Walt Wesley, produced four young players in return including Elmore Smith, Brian Winters, Dave Meyers and Junior Bridgeman.

But it wasn't until Coach Don Nelson arrived early in the 1976–77 season that the franchise turned around. He built around young players such as Bridgeman, Marques Johnson, Quinn Buckner and Sidney Moncrief. Later, veterans like Bob Lanier helped carry the Bucks through a period of seven straight seasons with 50 or more victories. Although they continually ran into the Philadelphia 76ers and Boston Celtics in the playoffs, Milwaukee remained one of the league's most successful franchises.

ROLL OF HONOR

Conference/Division	Eastern/Central			
First NBA year	1968–69			
Home Arena details	Bradley Center (built 1988, capacity 18,633)			
Former cities/nicknames	None			
NBA Championships	1971			
Playing Record	**G**	**W**	**L**	**Pct**
Regular Season	2460	1340	1120	.545
Playoffs (Series 16–18)	169	85	84	.503

GLENN ROBINSON
The Bucks' Big Dog

Former Milwaukee Bucks general manager Mike Dunleavy knew the future had arrived when he used the No. 1 overall pick in the 1994 NBA Draft to select Glenn Robinson.

An unusually intense and gifted small forward, Robinson brought the kind of scoring and rebounding skills Dunleavy's young Bucks had been missing. And Robinson, nicknamed "Big Dog," hasn't disappointed.

The 6–9 forward immediately became Milwaukee's primary scoring threat from anywhere on the court. Not only can he move outside and drain three-pointers, but Robinson is even more dangerous around the basket. Robinson's quickness and leaping ability make him virtually impossible to stop in the paint. All of which helped turn the Bucks into a playoff contender in 1995.

But it's Robinson's work ethic that could turn him into one of the league's brightest stars.

"He works extremely hard," says Dunleavy. "And he's only going to get better."

Despite missing all of training camp, Robinson's often spectacular rookie season landed him on the NBA All-Rookie First Team. He remains one of the league's best scoring forwards.

In the early 1990s, the team's fortunes took a downturn. The Bucks hit bottom and were forced to rebuild through the NBA Draft. Power forward Vin Baker and small forward Glenn "Big Dog" Robinson were acquired through the Draft, and each had an immediate impact. Baker was an All-Star by 1996, while Robinson was named to the 1996 U.S. Olympic team.

Baker was traded to Seattle prior to the 1997–98 season, but the three-team deal netted Milwaukee a top-notch point guard in the Cleveland Cavaliers' Terrell Brandon. With the emergence of shooting guard Ray Allen as a second scoring threat, the Bucks' offense has a new dimension for defenders to ponder. Solid play from veterans forwards like Armon Gilliam and Tyrone Hill give coach Chris Ford many weapons in the battle for an NBA Playoff berth.

LEFT: Glenn Robinson fires off a no-look pass.
RIGHT: Flying Buck: Milwaukee's Terrell Brandon goes over Sonic Gary Payton's attempted block.

Those Howling Wolves

It took 29 years, but Minnesota finally found its way back into the NBA with the Timberwolves. The Minneapolis Lakers won five championships in that city before moving to Los Angeles in 1960. The void was filled when the Timberwolves joined the NBA as an expansion team in 1989. Now all the Timberwolves have to do is win enough to make locals forget about the Lakers.

After eight losing seasons, three coaches and several front office changes, the Minnesota Timberwolves are still trying to find their trail to success in the NBA. Minnesota has lost an average of 58 games a season, hardly the performance Timberwolves fans had expected in a city that produced one of the most successful franchises in NBA history.

In the 1940s and 1950s, Minneapolis was the home of the Lakers. Those Laker teams won five NBA titles in six years before moving to Los Angeles in 1960. So fans in Minneapolis, a group that includes Mikan, met their new team with a clear sense of expectation. Two local businessmen, Harvey Ratner and Marv Wolfenson, were awarded the franchise in April, 1987.

What followed was a painstaking process of building the ideal franchise. But some early decisions, particularly the hiring of

Young Timberwolf Stephon Marbury is one of the quickest players in the NBA.

one-time University of Minnesota coach Bill Musselman, backfired. Musselman's teams won games, but he was criticized for failing to develop the young talent and was dismissed. He left in his second season and was replaced by former player Sidney Lowe.

Christian Laettner was drafted in 1992 and the 6–11 forward had an outstanding rookie season, averaging 18.2 points and 8.7 rebounds. Before the 1992–93 season, the team traded for forward Chuck Person and point guard Micheal Williams.

The new players were expected to give the team versatility and veteran leadership. But neither Person nor Williams shot very well and Minnesota's slow-paced offense found-ered as the team finished last in the league.

The 1993–94 season opened with measured optimism with the additions of high-scoring rookie guard Isaiah Rider and veteran forward Mike Brown. Bill Blair, a veteran NBA assistant coach, took over the team at the start of the 1994–95 season. In early 1995, the Timberwolves decided to build around Laettner and Rider by trading youth for experience. Rookie Donyell Marshall was dealt to Golden State for veteran Tom Gugliotta. In May 1995, the Timberwolves turned to Minnesota native Kevin McHale to be the architect of their building effort.

McHale made bold moves in attempting to put some teeth into the Wolves' attack. He started by drafting Kevin Garnett, a power forward who jumped to the NBA

ROLL OF HONOR

Conference/Division	Western/Midwest			
First NBA year	1989–90			
Home Arena details	Target Center (built 1990, capacity 19,006)			
Former cities/nicknames	None			
NBA Championships	None			
Playing Record	G	W	L	Pct
Regular Season	738	237	501	.321
Playoffs (Series 0–2)	8	2	6	.250

★ ★ ★ ★ ★ ★ ★ ★ ★ ★ ★

KEVIN GARNETT
Growing Up in the NBA

After their senior year of high school, most top basketball prospects are deciding which college to attend. Kevin Garnett chose to eliminate that step altogether and start his NBA career at the tender age of 19.

The 6–10, 220-pound power forward became the latest in a short line of NBA players with no college experience. One of the greatest centers in NBA history, Moses Malone, and Seattle power forward Shawn Kemp each became stars without any college experience. However, not every high school phenom who chose the NBA over college was so lucky.

Despite the odds against him, Garnett entered the 1995 NBA Draft after his senior year at Chicago's Farragut Academy. He was chosen fifth overall by the Wolves and became the youngest player in the NBA. Was he ready? Yes.

Garnett struggled briefly as he adjusted to life on the NBA road. Then he proved himself worthy of being in the league.

By his second full season, Garnett was worthy of an NBA All-Star selection with his combination of athleticism and court smarts.

"He's got the complete package," says Kevin McHale, the former Celtics great and current Minnesota VP of basketball operations. "He's going to be a force in this league."

after his senior year of high school. He then traded Laettner to Atlanta after the forward and Garnett had a falling out. Garnett's status as the team's leader was cemented when the Wolves acquired point guard Stephon Marbury, the No. 4 selection in the 1996 NBA Draft, in a draft-day swap with Milwaukee.

Marbury's arrival helped his close friend Garnett blossom into an All-Star in just his second season and, in each of Marbury's two seasons, the Wolves reached the NBA Playoffs. With Garnett redefining the forward position, Minnesota should be a postseason factor for many years to come.

Over the top: Kevin Garnett helped Minnesota into its first playoffs at the eighth attempt.

Looking for Respect

The glory years came and went with Julius Erving and the old American Basketball Association. Since entering the NBA in 1976, the Nets have moved from New York to New Jersey, yet they remain overshadowed by the New York Knicks. Coach John Calipari is now charged with forging an identity for the Nets, who feature young stars Kerry Kittles and Keith Van Horn.

They played their first games inside a dingy Armory just across the Hudson River from the bright lights of New York City. And despite moving all around New York and New Jersey before finding a lasting home in the Meadowlands at East Rutherford, the Nets survived, indeed thrived with a constantly changing roster that at one time or another has included some of the greatest players in basketball history.

The Nets were born out of the ABA's notion that no real sports league could survive without a strong franchise in the New York area. But during 1967–68, the Nets had to forfeit one home game because of water on the Armory floor. Another game had to be moved to a high school gym because of scheduling conflicts with a circus.

Within a year, the Nets had moved to Commack Arena on Long Island where they nearly self-destructed. A 17–61 season sent the franchise in a spin that didn't stop until businessman Roy Boe bought the team. He made three moves that turned the franchise around. Boe signed Coach Lou Carneseca, moved the team to Island Garden Arena, also on Long Island, and traded a first-round draft pick and a bundle of cash to the struggling Virginia franchise for Rick Barry.

Barry, one of the greatest scorers in professional basketball history, became the franchise's first true superstar. Barry led the Nets to the 1972 ABA Finals before near disaster struck again. A federal judge ordered Barry back to his former NBA team, the Golden State Warriors, for whom Barry had originally signed out of college.

After yet another arena move, to the Nassau Coliseum, the Nets found salvation once more in the struggling Squires. One the most lopsided deals in basketball history sent young Julius Erving to the Nets.

With former NBA player Kevin Loughery coaching the team, Erving led the Nets to two ABA titles and helped put the entire league on the basketball map. Indeed, the Nets were one of only four ABA teams to survive and join the NBA. The franchise, however, would never be the same. A complicated and controversial deal sent Erving to Philadelphia and the Nets back to the drawing board. In 1977, after yet another arena switch, temporarily to Piscataway, N.J. (until the Meadowlands Arena was completed), the team became the New Jersey Nets.

But NBA success, which came during the 1992–93 season under the direction of former Detroit and Dream Team coach Chuck Daly, was not without disappointment. The Nets finished 43–39 and came within a game of upsetting Cleveland in the first round of the playoffs. Daly was gone within two years, however, as were power forward Derrick Coleman and point guard Kenny Anderson. The trio were expected to lead the Nets to the NBA's promised land, but

ROLL OF HONOR

Conference/Division	Eastern/Atlantic			
First NBA year	1976–77 (ABA 1967–68)			
Home Arena details	Continental Airlines Arena (built 1981, cap. 20,029)			
Former cities/nicknames	New Jersey Americans (1967–68),			
	New York Nets (1968–77)			
NBA Championships	None (ABA — 1974, 1976)			

Playing Record	G	W	L	Pct
NBA Regular Season	1804	729	1075	.404
NBA/ABA combined	2548	1103	1445	.433
Playoffs (Series 1–10)	39	9	30	.231
NBA/ABA combined	108	46	62	.426

they all wore out their welcome in New Jersey. In 1995, Coleman went to the 76ers, while Anderson ended up in Charlotte.

The Nets have been rebuilding ever since Daly, Coleman and Anderson departed, but they are now heading in the right direction. Coach John Calipari has brought a renewed energy to the team. Rebounding master Jayson Williams has been joined by young talent like swingman Kerry Kittles and athletic forward Keith Van Horn. Throw in veteran guard Sam Cassell and the Nets had the formula for a return to the playoffs in 1997–98. As the young stars continue to grow, watch for the Nets to earn a healthy dose of respect over the next few seasons.

KEITH VAN HORN
Great Expectations

Keith Van Horn had yet to lace up his sneakers for his first NBA game when the comparisons started. Was he the next Larry Bird? Yes, the 6–10, 220-pound California native has similarities to Bird: Both have power forward size and small forward skills. But Van Horn doesn't think it's fair to compare him to the Boston legend now coaching in Indiana.

"I think people will realize that I'm a different player. He's more of a passer. I have more of a scoring mentality. He's a little wiser, smarter. I'm a little more athletic. I think people may compare us but once they see us as players, there will be some differences," says Van Horn, who arrived in New Jersey in a draft day trade after being the No. 2 selection in the 1997 NBA Draft.

In reality, New Jersey would be perfectly happy if Van Horn turned out like Chicago's Toni Kukoc—too fast for power forwards to defend, too big for small forwards to stop. Van Horn has excellent court skills to go with explosive leaping ability. He dominated on the college level at Utah, and his NBA future looks equally bright.

Picture of poise: His face a mask of total concentration, New Jersey's Kerry Kittles is perfectly balanced as he releases a jump shot against the Phoenix Suns.

Another Garden Party

The Knicks won their first two NBA championships in 1970 and 1973, events that turned Madison Square Garden into one of the loudest arenas on earth. Superstar Patrick Ewing now dominates on the court, and the Garden has started rocking again as the team looks for another championship with bright young stars like Allan Houston and Larry Johnson now roaming the Garden.

It might have been the most intelligent basketball team ever to play the game, and after 48 professional seasons it's the one team New York Knicks fans have never forgotten.

A group of players that included a future United State Senator (Bill Bradley) and three future NBA head coaches (Phil Jackson, Dave DeBusschere and Willis Reed) came together in the early 1970s to produce the only two championships for a franchise that played its first professional game in 1946.

With legendary coach Red Holzman calling the shots, the Knicks destroyed opponents with a combination of skill, tenacity and discipline. They played team defense and spread the ball around an offense that had scorers at every position.

Bradley and DeBusschere manned the

Larry Johnson looks for an open teammate.

forward spots, Reed played center and Walt Frazier, the flashy 6–4 guard, ran the show from out front. Jackson, who would win three NBA championships as coach of the Chicago Bulls, was a defensive stopper off the bench and known for his unselfish play.

Cazzie Russell and Dick Barnett played key roles on the 1970 Championship team while Earl Monroe, a dazzling ball handler and scorer, and Jerry Lucas came aboard for the 1973 title run. Those teams not only left a lasting impression on New Yorkers, but 20 years later Jackson applied many of Holzman's principles as coach of the Bulls.

Organized in 1946, the Knicks had a small but exciting lineup under another legendary coach, Joe Lapchick. Though the Knicks produced a string of solid seasons, they were no match for George Mikan and the Minneapolis Lakers. New York won three straight Eastern Division titles only to be defeated by Mikan's Lakers in three times in the Finals.

After that, New York didn't win a single playoff game between 1957 and 1967. But all that changed when Holzman took over midway through the 1967–68 season as he quickly molded the Knicks into an Eastern power. A championship roster came together as DeBusschere arrived via trade and Bradley returned after two years of study at Oxford. Reed had already established himself as a solid center and

ROLL OF HONOR				
Conference/Division	Eastern/Atlantic			
First NBA year	1946–47			
Home Arena details	Madison Square Garden (built 1968, capacity 19,763)			
Former cities/nicknames	None			
NBA Championships	1970, 1973			
Playing Record	G	W	L	Pct
Regular Season	4047	2079	1968	.514
Playoffs (Series 35–34)	309	156	153	.505

Frazier, only a rookie on Holzman's first team, would soon become one of the NBA's greatest defensive players.

When Bill Russell retired after leading Boston to its 11th title in 13 years following the 1968–69 season, the Eastern Conference became a wide open race with the Knicks perfectly positioned. They beat Wilt Chamberlain's Los Angeles Lakers for the 1970 Championship and then won again in 1973. But as the core players aged and injuries mounted, the Knicks headed into a period of inconsistency and almost constant change.

Between 1987 and 1992, New York had six head coaches in six seasons. Superstar center Patrick Ewing, the Knicks' No. 1 pick in the 1985 Draft, pushed the team to the brink of major playoff success in 1989 and 1990 only to see the franchise slip again.

But everyone seemed to know the Knicks were about to rise again. With Ewing, one of the most versatile centers ever to play the game, manning the middle, New York needed only to fill the edges.

Before the Knicks front office worried about players, however, the team decided to find a master tactician. This time the Knicks turned to another legendary coach in Pat Riley, whose Los Angeles Lakers had won four titles during the 1980s. Riley took control of a team led by Ewing, bruising power forward Charles Oakley and sharp-shooting guard John Starks. And upon Michael Jordan's brief retirement, the Eastern Conference was wide open again, and the Knicks took perfect advantage.

Led by Ewing, New York charged into the 1994 Finals only to lose a seven-game struggle with the Houston Rockets. But Riley shocked the club by resigning soon after New York's 1995 Eastern Conference Semifinal defeat by Indiana.

Under coach Jeff Van Gundy, the Knicks rebuilt Ewing's supporting cast. Guard Allan Houston and forward Larry Johnson added scoring punch, while Oakley was dealt to Toronto for shot-blocking young forward Marcus Camby. With these additions, New York has a versatile lineup and Ewing still has a good shot at an NBA Championship.

Patrick Ewing at the free-throw line.

WALT FRAZIER
A Style All His Own

With long black sideburns and a thick mustache, Walt "Clyde" Frazier carried himself with a style that was his alone. No one dressed better than Frazier. No one had more shoes, "kicks" as he called them, or hats, known as "lids" to Frazier. His suits were colorful and among the finest made, as were his ties ("knots").

On the floor, Frazier rarely changed expressions. His 6–4, 205-pound body seemed perfectly proportioned and always under control.

A first round draft pick in 1967 by the Knicks, Frazier had been an all-around star at Southern Illinois University. Frazier made the NBA All-Defensive first team seven straight seasons starting in 1969. By 1970, his third year in the league, Frazier had become one of the cornerstones to the NBA's best team.

Given Frazier's style, the title of his first book, *Rockin' Steady*, seemed only fitting.

Penny From Heaven

Orlando struggled through its first three seasons before Shaquille O'Neal appeared. With O'Neal's arrival in 1992, the Magic improved by 20 games over the previous season. In 1994–95, with another young star on board in Anfernee "Penny" Hardaway and a veteran power forward in Horace Grant, Orlando looked like a dynasty in the making. But O'Neal has moved on, leaving the team's future in Hardaway's hands.

Magic. The name fits. How else does a rising franchise end up with consecutive No. 1 Draft picks in a Lottery system weighted toward the league's worst teams?

A year after landing Shaquille O'Neal in the 1992 NBA Draft, the Magic won 41 games but ended one win short of the play-offs. Orlando went back into the league's Draft Lottery with by far the best record of the 11 non-playoff teams, and, given the nature of the lottery, it had a 1-in-66 chance of ending up with the top pick yet again.

But it happened. Despite achieving a .500 mark, Orlando was rewarded with yet another No. 1 draft choice. They chose Chris Webber, who was summarily dealt to Golden State for multi-talented guard Anfernee Hardaway plus three No. 1 picks. It led to a restructuring of the Lottery system, but the Magic had cashed in twice and, in the process, solidified the future.

All that was fine with front office dynamo Pat Williams, who had already provided

Horace Grant helped make Orlando a contender.

the franchise with a solid foundation. One of the NBA's finest promoters, Williams arrived in Orlando after a nearly 20-year education that started with the Chicago Bulls in 1969. In the mid-1980s, he departed to help bring a franchise to an Orlando community known primarily as the home to Disney World.

Williams' magic helped land one of four new expansion franchises and the team began play, along with Minnesota, in 1989. Not unexpectedly, Orlando struggled through a difficult first season, losing 64 games with aging veterans such as Reggie Theus, Sidney Green and Dave Corzine occupying roster spots.

The Magic improved quickly, however, behind young and talented players such as Dennis Scott and Nick Anderson. But a series of injuries buried Orlando during the 1991–92 season and the team lost 61 games, the NBA's second worst record.

The silver lining turned out to be the 1992 Draft which featured one of the most imposing centers in years in O'Neal. At 7–1 and 301 pounds, he had the ability and presence to redirect an entire franchise. And that's what O'Neal did, averaging 23.4 points, 13.8 rebounds and more than three blocked shots per game in his first NBA season. That was only the beginning. Hardaway added yet another dimension to a fast-rising franchise. Then, what many considered the final piece arrived when Horace Grant signed with the Magic. Orlando ended 1994–95 with the Eastern Conference's best record, and went to the 1995 NBA Finals. However, Houston swept the Magic in four straight games.

O'Neal took his Shaq Attack to the Lakers after the 1996 playoffs, leaving Hardaway

R O L L O F H O N O R				
Conference/Division	Eastern/Atlantic			
First NBA year	1989–90			
Home Arena details	Orlando Arena (built 1989, capacity 15,291)			
Former cities/nicknames	None			
NBA Championships	None			
Playing Record	G	W	L	Pct
Regular Season	738	364	374	.493
Playoffs (Series 5–4)	41	20	21	.488

HORACE GRANT
Three Ring Leader

Until Horace Grant arrived in Orlando prior to the 1994–95 season, Shaquille O'Neal had a problem. Try as he might, not even O'Neal could control the Magic's inside game by himself. And although O'Neal and the rest of the young Orlando roster had improved dramatically, the team still needed a veteran to show the way.

Enter Grant.

After helping the Chicago Bulls to three consecutive championships with his solid defense and rebounding, Grant signed with Orlando as a free agent in 1994. That move, coupled with Orlando's improved play, turned the franchise into an instant championship contender.

Not only does Grant know how to win in the playoffs, something the Magic hadn't done prior to 1995, but he has become the perfect complement to O'Neal under the basket. Grant gives Orlando another rebounder, but it's his defense that stands out.

"Horace understands the importance of defense," says former Bulls coach John Bach. "And he's not afraid of doing what it takes to get the job done."

In 1994, Grant was named to the NBA All-Defensive Second Team.

in control of the Magic's destiny. Orlando coaxed coach Chuck Daly, who led Detroit to two titles and the Dream Team to Olympic glory, out of retirement.

Persistent injuries to Hardaway kept Orlando from the NBA Playoffs in the 1997–98 campaign, but bright spots included a resurgent Anderson at shooting guard and the energetic contributions of forward Bo Outlaw. With two lottery picks in the 1998 NBA Draft, don't count the Magic out of the NBA Championship hunt.

Worth Every Penny: Hardaway has three Suns defenders in his wake as he flies to the basket.

Looking for Another House Call

The Philadelphia 76ers rode Julius "Dr. J" Erving's brilliance to the 1983 NBA Championship. But after trading superstar Charles Barkley and revamping the roster from the bottom up, Philadelphia has turned the future over to Allen Iverson and coach Larry Brown. If the 76ers are going to rekindle title hopes, they'll have to do it with those two leading the way.

Allen Iverson delivers a sweet dish.

The Philadelphia 76ers have done just about everything at least once. From winning NBA titles to recording the single worst season in league history and trading away two of basketball's most accomplished players, Philadelphia has long been one of the NBA's more colorful creations.

The team started out as the Syracuse Nationals, arriving in Philadelphia in 1963. Indeed, the 76ers were born out of the void created by the Philadelphia Warriors' move to San Francisco. Since then, the 76ers have usually been one of the league's foremost attractions for one reason or another.

The franchise is also considered largely responsible for the creation of the 24-second clock. In an intrasquad game prior to the 1954–55 season, Syracuse owner Danny Biasone improvised an early forerunner of the current shot clock. He decided on 24 seconds as an experimental time guide for offensive possessions. The experiment proved to be a success and the NBA adopted Biasone's idea as a league rule, which resulted in a faster, more high-scoring game.

The early Syracuse teams also had two of the era's finest players, Dolph Schayes and Johnny "Red" Kerr. With the addition of rookie Earl Lloyd for the 1954–55 season, the Nationals won their only championship.

Once in Philadelphia, however, the franchise became a league-wide show. San Francisco grudgingly agreed to trade Wilt Chamberlain to the 76ers midway through the 1964–65 season. A year later, the 76ers had a starting lineup loaded with talent. Chamberlain, Chet Walker, Hal Greer, Billy Cunningham and Wali Jones helped the 76ers to a brilliant 68–13 regular season record, the fourth best in history.

With Chamberlain passing more than earlier in his career, Philadelphia ended Boston's string of eight straight NBA titles by eliminating the Celtics in the playoffs. The 76ers went on to beat San Francisco in the 1967 Finals for their first Philadelphia title.

Less than two years later, however, Chamberlain was sent to the Lakers and the 76ers self-destructed. They lost a record 73 games during the 1972–73 season. But within four years the team again had one of the most exciting rosters in the league with Julius

ROLL OF HONOR

Conference/Division	Eastern/Atlantic			
First NBA year	1949–50			
Home Arena details	Core States Center (built 1996, capacity 21,000)			
Former cities/nicknames	Syracuse Nationals (1949–63)			
NBA Championships	1955, 1967, 1983			

Playing Record	G	W	L	Pct
Regular Season	3876	2088	1788	.539
Playoffs (Series 36–34)	328	175	153	.534

Erving, George McGinnis, Steve Mix, Doug Collins and Darryl Dawkins carrying Philadelphia into the 1977 NBA Finals.

Behind Erving's brilliant play and the coaching of Cunningham, the 76ers were one of the elite teams in the league in the early 1980s. The era produced only a single title (1983), however, as the Lakers and Celtics started to dominate.

Charles Barkley arrived in 1984 and the 76ers remained a solid team capable of beating anyone. But Erving eventually slowed down and Philadelphia slowed with him. Following Barkley's trade in 1992 the 76ers lost 56 games.

The future, as far as owner Harold Katz believed, arrived in 1993. Philadelphia used the No. 2 pick to select 7–6 center Shawn Bradley, who was given uniform No. 76. But the Bradley era was short-lived, as he did not live up to his potential and was sent to New Jersey for Derrick Coleman. The Sixers were energized by the selection of point guard Allen Iverson with the No. 1 pick in the 1996 NBA Draft. Iverson backed up his brash on-court image with consistently thrilling performances en route to winning the 1997 NBA Rookie of the Year award.

The 1997–98 season brought veteran coach Larry Brown to town, and the 76ers made several moves to improve the team. Gone was Stackhouse, but the team added athletic forwards Tim Thomas, Joe Smith and Theo Ratliff. The resurgent Coleman sparkled for the Sixers, and Iverson continued to show signs of superstardom. With some seasoning, Brown's squad could return the 76ers to the glory days of Dr. J.

Tim Thomas flying to the basket.

Home of the Rising Suns

For years the Phoenix Suns had been one of the Western Conference's top teams. They even made an appearance in the 1976 NBA Finals. But the Suns never won more than 57 regular season games until Charles Barkley rode into town prior to the 1992–93 season. The Suns won a franchise-record 62 games and reached the 1993 Finals, this time losing to Chicago. The Suns have risen, but can they finally win a championship?

For years the first pick in the NBA Draft was determined by the simple toss of a coin. Representatives from the worst teams in the Eastern and Western Conferences would gather for the coin flip.

As the Phoenix Suns can attest, being lucky usually translates into being good. The Suns entered the league along with Milwaukee in 1968. Both teams limped through difficult first seasons, Phoenix relying on sharp shooting guards Gail Goodrich and Dick Van Arsdale and not much else. In the East, the Bucks had similar problems.

As a result, the Suns and Bucks squared off in the coin toss. This one, however, had historic implications that both franchises understood. The Suns called heads. The coin came up tails, Lew Alcindor (now Kareem Abdul-Jabbar) went to Milwaukee and within two seasons the Bucks had an NBA title.

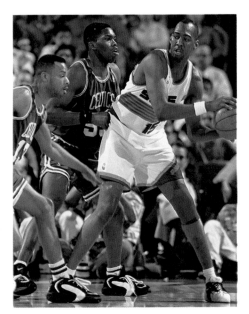

Danny Manning ready for action.

ROLL OF HONOR

Conference/Division	Western/Pacific			
First NBA year	1968–69			
Home Arena details	America West Arena (dedicated 1992, capacity 19,023)			
Former cities/nicknames	None			
NBA Championships	None			
Playing Record	**G**	**W**	**L**	**Pct**
Regular Season	2460	1342	1118	.546
Playoffs (Series 20–20)	185	90	95	.486

COTTON FITZSIMMONS
Never Say Goodbye

At the end of the 1992 season, Cotton Fitzsimmons turned over the job of Phoenix coach to his assistant, Paul Westphal. Fitzsimmons thought his coaching days were done. He was wrong.

Fitzsimmons found himself back on the Phoenix bench midway through the 1995–96 season when Westphal was dismissed and he guided the Suns into the playoffs.

Fitzsimmons' return to coaching came 26 years after his first year as an NBA coach—with the Suns, of course. Along the way he also coached in Atlanta, Buffalo, Kansas City and San Antonio.

The 66-year-old Fitzsimmons turned the coaching duties over to Danny Ainge at the beginning of the 1996–97 season, returning to a front-office position with the Suns. When it comes to coaching in Phoenix, however, Fitzsimmons has learned to never say never.

What about the Suns? It has been a struggle often with narrow playoff defeats. But just a year after that inaugural season, Phoenix extended the Los Angeles Lakers to seven games in the Western Division semifinals,

a remarkable turnaround aided by playground legend Connie Hawkins.

Although it took six years for Phoenix to reach the playoffs again, the building process remained impressive. By 1976 the team had assembled the best team in the West with young stars such as Paul Westphal, Alvan Adams, Garfield Heard and Curtis Perry and veterans Van Arsdale and Keith Erickson.

A 42–40 regular season finish set up a dramatic postseason that included what many think is the best playoff game in NBA history. Phoenix beat Seattle in the conference semifinals and then upset defending champion Golden State to reach the Finals.

And that's where the real drama began. Matched against the Boston Celtics, the Suns won two of the first four games to set up a crucial Game 5 at Boston. The contest took three overtime periods and rolled along at a numbing pace. It took Heard's incredible, high-arching jump shot with one second left in the second overtime to force yet a third extra period. Ultimately, Boston's deep bench and veteran cool prevailed and the Celtics went on to close out the title in six games.

But the Suns had established themselves under coach John MacLeod. Players such as Westphal, Adams and Walter Davis made Phoenix one of the West's top teams for years. But the Suns didn't make a return trip to the Finals until Charles Barkley arrived in 1992. With Westphal becoming coach and Barkley taking over scoring and rebounding, the Suns rolled through the 1992–93 season. Phoenix was only derailed by Chicago in the NBA Finals.

Barkley left in 1996, a potentially disastrous move for Phoenix. The Suns started 0–13, but new coach Danny Ainge wouldn't give up. He rallied his team, which benefitted from the midseason acquisition of 1995 co-Rookie of the Year Jason Kidd. Ainge, a former Phoenix guard, cooked up a four-guard rotation to emphasize the Suns' strength at that position and downplay the team's lack of size.

After another playoff appearance in 1997–98, Johnson and Phoenix parted ways. Despite the loss of their longtime point guard and continuing knee problems for versatile forward Danny Manning, Ainge and the Suns remain one of the NBA's most exciting teams.

One of the most creative playmakers, Jason Kidd knows how to break down a defense.

BLAZERS

One Brief Shining Moment

It happened in 1977 when center Bill Walton found the strength and physical good fortune to last an entire season. The Trail Blazers won the only championship in franchise history, an improbable romp past the Philadelphia 76ers. Since then, however, near misses on and off the court have left Portland looking for yet another chance.

Despite years of success and two recent trips to the NBA Finals, the Portland franchise is marked by two events that came seven years apart.

The first happened in 1977 when the Trail Blazers led by center Bill Walton and forward Maurice Lucas marched through an unlikely yet brilliant playoff run en route to the franchise's only NBA Championship.

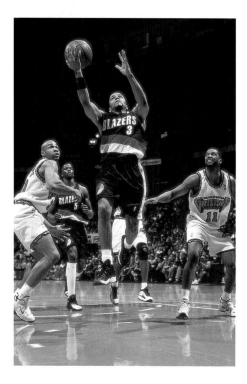

Coming home: Damon Stoudamire left Toronto to play for his hometown Portland Trail Blazers.

The team had joined the NBA in 1971 along with expansion franchises in Buffalo and Cleveland. Lenny Wilkens took over the coaching duties in 1974, which was also his last season as a player.

Wilkens lasted two seasons before management turned the team over to Jack Ramsay. A great coach in his own right, Ramsay received the gift of his career when Walton stayed healthy enough to last through the 1976–77 season.

Teamed with Lucas and a rag-tag collection of hard-working players, Walton turned the Trail Blazers into champions. Walton led the league in rebounding (14.4) and blocked shots (3.25) and his passing helped ignite the league's third best offense.

But after breezing through the first three rounds of the 1976 playoffs, Portland ran hard into Julius Erving and the Philadelphia 76ers in the Finals. Philadelphia took a quick 2–0 lead and as the series shifted to Portland, many thought the Trail Blazers were quite simply overmatched.

That's when Portland exploded, winning the next two games by 22 and 32 points and forever shifting the momentum. The Trail Blazers went on to win four straight games and claim their first and only NBA title. The championship run not only shocked the rest of the league, but it make a folk hero out of Walton.

Able to defend, pass and score as well as any big man in the league, Walton appeared to be the kind of player that could carry an

BILL WALTON
Two Feet Short

The pain in Bill Walton's feet could be felt throughout the entire NBA. One of the greatest college players in the history of basketball, Walton figured to be at least that good as a professional.

He could shoot, defend, run the floor and pass as well as any big man in the game. So when Portland acquired Walton in the 1974 Draft, the league took notice.

Though Walton's performance never disappointed, his body failed miserably. Foot injuries limited him to 35 games as a rookie and just 51 games his second season. Walton stayed healthy enough to play 65 games during the 1976–77 season, however, and then carried on through the playoffs.

Walton averaged 18.2 points, 15.2 rebounds, blocked more than three shots a game and helped direct the Portland offense. The Trail Blazers overcame Philadelphia to win the 1977 NBA Championship.

Although Walton's career would continue to be marked by injuries, he did win another NBA title with Boston in 1986.

By the 1997–98 season, Portland had completely reinvented itself. With Mike Dunleavy in the coaching seat and hometown hero Damon Stoudamire running the point, the Blazers featured a powerful offense with players like swingman Isaiah Rider, forwards Walt Williams and Rasheed Wallace, and Lithuanian center Arvydas Sabonis. This group led the franchise to a 16th consecutive playoff berth, setting its sights on another NBA title for Blazers fans.

ABOVE Brian Grant: At full stretch. RIGHT Arvydas Sabonis: Lithuanian lift-off.

entire franchise. Once considered a solid but thin team, Portland was now seen as a team on the rise with a potentially dominating player leading the ascension.

Portland was even better the following season, but Walton's foot problems ended any chance of another title. His season ended two games into the playoffs and eventually, so too did his future in Portland. Walton missed the entire 1978–79 season and a year later was shipped off to the San Diego Clippers.

Portland had a chance to take another giant leap forward in 1984. A previous trade had given Portland, 48–34 in the 1983–84 season, the No. 2 pick in the 1984 Draft.

But with it came a decision that will forever haunt the franchise. After Houston selected Hakeem Olajuwon with the first choice, Portland decided to gamble on 7–1 center Sam Bowie. Chicago then used the third pick to grab Michael Jordan.

With a young Clyde Drexler set to take over the shooting guard spot and Kiki Vandweghe the team's leading scorer at small forward, Portland lacked only a solid big man in the middle.

But Bowie had missed two entire seasons during college at the University of Kentucky with leg problems. Though no one figured Jordan would become the game's brightest star, everyone knew about Bowie's medical problems. And Portland paid dearly for what turned out to be a horrible mistake. Bowie missed 44 games his second season, 77 his third and then didn't play at all his fourth year in the league.

As with Walton, however, Portland survived Bowie's injuries. Indeed, the franchise corrected itself quickly and entered the 1990s as the West's dominant team. Led by Drexler, Terry Porter, Jerome Kersey and Buck Williams, the Trail Blazers reached the NBA Finals in 1990 and 1992 but lost hard-fought championship rounds to first Detroit and then Chicago.

Portland began to remake itself again before the 1994–95 season when P.J. Carlesimo took over as head coach. Then, in early 1995, Drexler was dealt to Houston.

ROLL OF HONOR

Conference/Division	Western/Pacific
First NBA year	1970–71
Home Arena details	Rose Garden (built 1995, capacity 21,538)
Former cities/nicknames	None
NBA Championships	1977

Playing Record	G	W	L	Pct
Regular Season	2296	1224	1072	.533
Playoffs (Series 14–20)	152	71	81	.467

The Traveling Kings

They have moved across the country with stops in Rochester, Cincinnati, Kansas City and finally Sacramento, but the Kings still haven't found the road to the NBA Finals. But since settling in Sacramento, the Kings have started to assemble a roster capable of making a run at the playoffs. In 1995–96, the Kings finally hit postseason paydirt.

Consider the cross-country odyssey that landed the Kings in Sacramento. It does provide perspective. The Sacramento Kings used to be the Kansas City Kings, who used to be the Kansas City-Omaha Kings, who used to be the Cincinnati Royals, who were originally the Rochester Royals. There was even a brief life before that in the Midwest.

If that's not enough, consider the disparate group of players on that first team. Future pro football Hall of Fame quarterback Otto Graham, eventual television star Chuck Connors, future New York Knicks coach Red Holzman and long-time

major league baseball player Del Rice were all members of the 1946 team that won the National Basketball League title. Not surprisingly, the team was located elsewhere, in Sheboygan, Wisconsin, during that championship season.

Rochester joined the NBA in 1948 and immediately became one of the strongest franchises. By their third season, the Royals were playing for the NBA title thanks to players such as Arnie Risen and Bob Davies.

The Royals, and later the Kings, would never reach another championship series. That might have changed had the career of Maurice Stokes not been cut short by tragedy. Stokes arrived in the 1955 Draft and was developing into a top player when he contracted a crippling brain disease called encephalitis.

A year earlier, in 1957, the team had moved to Cincinnati in part because management wanted to claim the great Oscar Robertson with a territorial pick in the 1960 Draft.

Robertson, star of the U.S. men's team in the 1960 Rome Olympics, joined the team for the 1960–61 season. Robertson averaged an incredible 30.8 points, 12.3 rebounds and 11.5 assists per game during the 1961–62 season. No player has even come close to averaging double figures in

Extreme close-up: Sacremento's Billy Owens is about to slam.

any three statistical categories, much less a player who stood 6–5 and played guard.

But not even Robertson could carry the Royals past Bill Russell's Boston Celtics.

From there, however, the franchise lapsed into a 26-year period marked by moves and mediocrity. It moved West and became the Kansas City-Omaha Kings and, four years later, the Kansas City Kings.

The team's only real playoff success came unexpectedly following the 1980–81 season. With Otis Birdsong, Scott Wedman and Phil Ford doing all the scoring, the Kings just made the playoffs with a 40–42 regular season record.

But after knocking off Portland in the First Round, the Kings shocked Pacific Division champion Phoenix in a rousing seven-game series. They were eventually eliminated by the Houston Rockets in the Western Conference finals.

By 1985 the Kings were on the move again, this time landing in Sacramento. The Kings appeared headed out of their dark age until injuries beat them down again.

More changes are in store for the Kings in the 1998–99 season. Longtime scoring leader Mitch Richmond was swapped to Washington for talented power forward Chris Webber. Webber joins a Sacramento squad that is suddenly deep in the frontcourt, with talented youngsters like Corliss Williamson and Michael Stewart joining veteran swingman Billy Owens.

The move to bring in Webber signals a new era in Kings history. Fans hope he will help the Kings finally take up permanent residency in the playoffs.

• •

Corliss Williamson takes off for the basket.

ROLL OF HONOR

Conference/Division	Western/Pacific		
First NBA year	1948–49		
Home Arena details	ARCO Arena (built 1988, capacity 17,317)		
Former cities/nicknames	Rochester Royals (1948–57), Cincinnati Royals (1957–72), Kansas-City-Omaha Kings (1972–75)		
NBA Championships	1951		

Playing Record	G	W	L	Pct
Regular Season	3941	1792	2149	.455
Playoffs (Series 9–20)	118	46	72	.390

A Tale of Two Players

Few teams won more creatively than the San Antonio Spurs of the late 1970s and early 1980s. They led the league in scoring by connecting from just about anywhere on the court. But they never reached a single championship series. Now the responsibility of carrying the franchise rests with 7–1 center David Robinson, a former Naval officer nicknamed "The Admiral," who has been joined by fellow center Tim Duncan.

They will be remembered as the two greatest players in the Spurs' history. Alas for San Antonio, by the time David Robinson and George Gervin ended on the same bench, one was playing while the other coached.

Look back to the league's most dominant championship teams and all of them had an inside-outside attack. Unfortunately for Robinson and Gervin, the two championship components never intersected. Gervin's brilliant 12-year career in San Antonio ended four years before Robinson arrived and so far, neither has an NBA title to show for all their wondrous talents.

The Spurs began as the Dallas Chaparrals in the ABA. Though Dallas had immediate success on the court, winning 46 games its first season, the franchise was a box office disaster. The team eventually became the Texas Chaparrals and alternated home games between Dallas, Fort Worth and Lubbock.

Then, in 1973, San Antonio businessman Red McCombs bought the franchise, moved it to his home town and renamed it the Spurs. Before the 1973–74 season, McCombs also spent more than $500,000, an enormous sum then, to buy Gervin and center Swen Nater from Virginia. Gervin, a slender 6–7 scoring machine, had a dazzling array of hooks, scoops, jumpers and dunks. By the time San Antonio joined the NBA in 1976, Gervin had four professional seasons behind him and a fully-developed offensive arsenal.

Gervin won four scoring titles in five years

Tower of power: San Antonio's Tim Duncan.

as the Spurs became one of the most explosive teams in history. But without an impact player at center, his heroics weren't enough. Conference Finals were reached under Coach Stan Albeck in 1982 and '83 but the Spurs were beaten by the Los Angeles Lakers.

San Antonio didn't return to form until Robinson arrived in 1989. The Spurs had used the No. 1 pick in 1987 to draft Robinson, who had to fulfill a military commitment before he could join the team.

When he arrived Robinson lived up to the

SEAN ELLIOTT
No Place Like Home

After four solid seasons in San Antonio—including one All-Star appearance—Sean Elliott was shocked when the Spurs traded him to Detroit for forward Dennis Rodman in 1993. Elliott, a sharp-shooting small forward, had found a home on the perimeter of the Spurs offense. When opposing defenses collapsed on David Robinson, Elliott was open for three-point bombs.

In Detroit, without a dominant big man, Elliott never found his stride. His 12.1 points in 1993–94 was his lowest average since his rookie year, and Elliott was miserable on a rebuilding team.

He longed to return to San Antonio, and the Pistons granted him his wish by sending him back to the Spurs after just one season. Rejuvinated, Elliott became an even bigger offensive factor in his second San Antonio stint. He became a more accurate three-point shooter and added a variety of slashing moves to the basket to his bag of tricks.

The Spurs appear to have learned their lesson. They aren't likely to part with Elliott again anytime soon.

expectations. Robinson not only helped San Antonio improve from 21 to 56 victories in his first season, but the Spurs narrowly

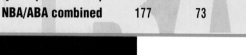

ROLL OF HONOR

Conference/Division	Western/Midwest		
First NBA year	1976–77 (ABA 1967–68)		
Home Arena details	Alamodome (built 1993, capacity 20,500)		
Former cities/nicknames	Dallas Chaparrals (1967–70, 1971–73),		
	Texas Chaparrals (1970–71)		
NBA Championships	None		

Playing Record	G	W	L	Pct
NBA Regular Season	1804	990	814	.549
NBA/ABA combined	2548	1356	1180	.535
NBA Playoffs (series 9–18)	128	56	71	.438
NBA/ABA combined	177	73	104	.412

missed the Western Conference Finals. Portland needed two overtime victories, the second in a grueling Game 7, to eliminate San Antonio in the 1990 Conference Semifinals.

It took time for the Spurs to return to that level. Injuries to starters Terry Cummings and Willie Anderson stunted the team's progress. Numerous coaching changes sent the franchise spinning until former player John Lucas took over 21 games into the 1992–93 campaign. Lucas immediately turned to Robinson, who carried San Antonio back to the Conference Semifinals. The team added Dennis Rodman prior to the 1993–94 season and Cummings and Anderson appeared recovered from their injuries. Then, prior to the 1994–95 season, Bob Hill took over as the team's head coach and Sean Elliott returned in a trade.

The Spurs responded by winning a club record 62 games and the Midwest Division title, while Robinson was named the NBA's MVP. The Spurs reached the Western Conference Finals before falling to Houston.

Injuries kept Robinson out of all but six games in 1996–97, crippling the Spurs' attack. The silver lining was the No. 1 pick in the 1997 NBA Draft, which the Spurs won in the draft lottery. With it, San Antonio plucked multitalented center Tim Duncan.

Duncan won NBA Rookie of the Year honors, and the Spurs surged back into the NBA Playoffs. With this pair of 7-footers in the middle, San Antonio hopes to tower over the opposition and earn an elusive championship.

The Admiral Takes Command: David Robinson throws down a lefthanded slam on the Bucks.

Blasting Off Again

The Seattle SuperSonics appeared to be on their way to a dubious distinction: best regular-season team in the NBA. Despite stellar seasons in 1994 and 1995, the Sonics had lost in the first round of the NBA Playoffs. All that changed in 1996, as Gary Payton led the Sonics to their first NBA Finals appearance since 1979.

The SuperSonics had made it to the Western Conference Finals in 1993, but couldn't duplicate their postseason success in the next three seasons. Seattle fans hope that their team will lead them to their first NBA Championship in nearly two decades.

Indeed, Coach George Karl can only hope the experience pays off like it did for Lenny Wilkens' squad. Wilkens, who had been a player/coach for Seattle in the early 1970s, returned to the bench early in the 1977–78 season and immediately transformed the franchise into a winner.

Seattle had come into the league in 1967, but had only limited success until Wilkens' arrival in 1969. As the Sonics' point guard, he guided the team to 47 victories during the 1971–72 season but, incredibly, the team failed to make the playoffs.

Former Boston great Bill Russell coached the team for four seasons and led Seattle to its first playoff appearance in 1975. But Russell's hard-edged approach didn't wear well. Before long, owner Sam Schulman was digging in his files for another leader.

That's where he found Wilkens, who had since retired as a player. Wilkens returned to his former team and quickly molded players such as Gus Williams, Jack Sikma, Dennis Johnson, Freddie Brown and Marvin Webster into a title contender.

The SuperSonics rolled through the early rounds of the playoffs before meeting Washington. A seven-game championship battle ended with the Bullets taking the 1978 championship on Seattle's home court, something no one forgot when the two teams met again a year later.

Although Webster, a towering center, left the team for New York following the Finals, the SuperSonics never missed a beat.

Vin Baker is playing at a different level.

They received bulky Lonnie Shelton from the Knicks as compensation for Webster and turned the center spot over to Sikma.

By the time the SuperSonics returned to the Finals in 1979 not even the Bullets had a chance. Seattle eliminated Washington in a quick five-game series for the franchise's first championship.

The team remained solid through the next 12 seasons, but never quite as good as it was under Wilkens. Players such as Tom Chambers, Xavier McDaniel and Dale Ellis helped keep the team competitive. Then, midway through the 1991–92 season, Coach George Karl took over and the SuperSonics' roster came together.

Combining veterans Eddie Johnson and Ricky Pierce with youngsters Shawn Kemp, Derrick McKey and Gary Payton, Karl

ROLL OF HONOR

Conference/Division	Western/Pacific			
First NBA year	1967–68			
Home Arena details	Key Arena (built 1995, capacity 17,800)			
Former cities/nicknames	None			
NBA Championships	1979			

Playing Record	G	W	L	Pct
Regular Season	2542	1371	1171	.539
Playoffs (Series 18–17)	175	84	91	.480

turned the SuperSonics into an end-to-end menace. Seattle traded for veteran center Sam Perkins just after the 1993 All-Star break and, suddenly, the SuperSonics were ready to make their run. Kemp, one of the NBA's rising superstars, averaged 17.8 points and more than 10 rebounds a game. But it was defense that keyed the Seattle charge as they became the only team in the league to finish among the top five in scoring and defense. The SuperSonics knocked off Utah and Houston before finally losing to Phoenix in the seventh game of the 1993 Western Conference Finals.

If Seattle learned anything it's that the team needed just a little more help, particularly in the starting lineup. In two quick, if not brilliant moves, the SuperSonics added 6–5 guard Kendall Gill in a trade with Charlotte and 6–10 forward Detlef Schrempf in a deal with Indiana.

Schrempf provided veteran leadership on the frontline, while Gill, among the league's most versatile guards, added another dimension out front. Both became perfect additions to the full-court attack that turned Seattle into the league's best team during the 1993–94 regular season. But a stunning loss to Denver in the First Round of the 1994 Playoffs ended a spectacular season. The same scenario was repeated in 1994–95 when a strong season ended in a first-round loss in the Playoffs. In 1995–96, Seattle broke out of its Playoff slump and surged to the NBA Finals, only to lose to Chicago 4–2.

Despite excellent showings in the regular season, the Sonics were unable to duplicate their 1996 NBA Finals showing in the following years. After the 1997 playoffs, Kemp was dealt away in a trade that brought Vin Baker to Seattle from Milwuakee. The young power forward blended well into the Sonics' style of play, but another second-round playoff exit brought an end to Karl's run as Seattle coach. The on-court talent remains, however, for the Sonics to storm back into the title chase.

DETLEF SCHREMPF
Back Home Again

The tattoo just over Detlef Schrempf's heart shows, among other things, an eagle spreading its wings. For Schrempf, the image has meaning. "It has more to do with inner strength," he says.

And that's something Schrempf knows about. After a solid career at the University of Washington, Schrempf was the first-round pick of the Dallas Mavericks in 1985. His style was supposed to be perfect for the rapidly rising Mavericks. Instead, Schrempf suffered through three disappointing seasons in Dallas before being traded to Indiana.

Schrempf blossomed into an All-Star in Indiana and twice was named the league's best Sixth Man. When he moved into the Pacers' starting lineup in 1992–93, he became an All-Star for the first time registering career bests in total rebounds, assists, points and steals.

By the time Schrempf was dealt to Seattle in 1993, he had become one of the league's best all-around players.

Super SuperSonic: Gary Payton.

Building on A History of Success

The Toronto Raptors were built around two guards—former Pistons great Isiah Thomas, the team's architect, and 1996 NBA Rookie of the Year Damon Stoudamire, the team's first draft choice. But both were gone by the end of the 1997–98 season, causing a still-new team to return to the drawing board with a group of talented forwards.

As a college sophomore, Isiah Thomas led Indiana University to the NCAA Championship. In the NBA, as one of the most dynamic point guards to ever play the game, Thomas guided Detroit to back-to-back NBA titles. So when Toronto team president John Bitove went looking for the man to lead the expansion Raptors, the decision was an easy one.

"The two things that came through over and over were that Thomas is incredibly intelligent and he's driven to be successful," says Bitove.

As vice president of basketball operations for the Raptors, Thomas used every ounce of experience he gained during his brilliant NBA career to make Toronto competitive. The Raptors, along with the Vancouver Grizzlies, made their NBA debut in the 1995–96 season, playing in the tough Central Division which includes teams such as the Chicago Bulls, Atlanta Hawks and Detroit Pistons.

That's one reason Thomas wasted no time before studying some of the most successful coaches and front office people in professional sports. He found out how coaches such as Don Shula of NFL's Miami Dolphins built that franchise into a power. And he talked to NBA veterans, including former Pistons coach Chuck Daly and all-time Boston Celtics great Bill Russell.

"It confirmed a gut feeling I had that being an expansion team, that if you wanted to win a championship and you depended strictly on the rules, then it's going to take you

Tracy McGrady bypassed college for the NBA.

a long time to do that," said Thomas. "You've got to be imaginative, be creative. The Dallas Cowboys, when they came in, started drafting basketball players, baseball players, people they looked at in a totally different paradigm. They made a shift in sports that football hadn't taken then. They had to change the game, the way people thought."

Which is exactly what Thomas did when Toronto made its first choice in the 1995 NBA Draft. Instead of drafting a big man with the No. 7 pick, Thomas defied conventional wisdom and chose point guard

Making the right move: Toronto's Doug Christie dribbles to the basket.

Damon Stoudamire. As it turned out, that was just one of many moves orchestrated by Thomas.

Former Chicago guard B.J. Armstrong was selected first by the Raptors in the expansion draft, but with the selection of Stoudamire, Armstrong was traded for some frontcourt players to add to veterans Oliver Miller, Ed Pinckney, John Salley, Zan Tabak, Dontonio Wingfield, Doug Smith, Jerome Kersey, Tony Massenburg and Acie Earl, all of whom were selected in the expansion draft. Others arriving through the expansion draft were Willie Anderson, B.J. Tyler, Keith Jennings and Andres Guibert.

Some of those players did not make it through the Raptors' first season, while some blossomed. Stoudamire outperformed all expectations, earning NBA Rookie of the Year honors. Toronto's second season saw an improvement to 30 wins and another good young player came through the draft in forward/center Marcus Camby, and he was joined by high school phenom small forward Tracy McGrady, a 1997 NBA Draft gamble by Thomas, but a player with a fine all-around game.

The 1997–98 season proved to be a turning point for the Raptors. Thomas left the team to become a TV analyst, while Stoudamire was traded to his hometown Portland Trail Blazers. After the season, the Raptors named Butch Carter to coach a team filled with dazzling young players such as McGrady and point guard Chauncey Billups. Camby was dealt away, but veteran big men Charles Oakley and Kevin Willis were acquired. Factor in the explosive rookie Vince Carter — the latest player to be tagged as "the next Michael Jordan" — and Toronto may be moving toward a winning future.

ROLL OF HONOR

Conference/Division	Eastern/Central			
First NBA year	1995–96			
Home Arena details	Air Canada Centre (built 1998, capacity 19,800)			
Former cities/nicknames	None			
NBA Championships	None			
Playing Record	G	W	L	Pct
Regular Season	246	67	179	.272
Playoffs	yet to qualify			

The Jazz Age

The name belongs to another city, but the results are Utah's alone. Riding the remarkable talents of superstars John Stockton and Karl Malone, the Jazz haven't missed the playoffs since 1983. But if Utah hopes to map out another championship run it's going to need more than a dynamic duo to get the job done.

I n a city best known for the Mormon Tabernacle, the nickname of the state's only major professional sports franchise doesn't fit. Then again, no one figured the New Orleans Jazz would one day be situated in Salt Lake City, Utah.

When the team became the NBA's 18th franchise in 1974 it was situated in New Orleans, a town known for its music as well as its 24-hour clubs. Given the sensibilities of the respective communities, the Jazz could not have endured a greater culture shock when the franchise moved to Utah in 1979.

But it had been a rocky start in New Orleans, where the team had five coaches in its first five seasons. Management had also gambled heavily on local legend "Pistol" Pete Maravich, one of the greatest showmen the game has ever known.

Maravich had become a college basket-ball legend at Louisiana State University and management, banking on Maravich's drawing power, wanted him back home. The Jazz put together an elaborate package of players and draft picks to obtain Maravich from the Atlanta Hawks for New Orleans' first season.

After a difficult debut, the Jazz quickly became respectable thanks in large part to Maravich. The 6–5 guard, who handled the ball as well as any player in history, was twice named to the All-NBA first team during his five seasons with the Jazz. Maravich led the league in scoring in 1976–77 and once drilled the New York Knicks for 68 points in a single game. But the Pistol wasn't

All That Jazz: John Stockton takes off.

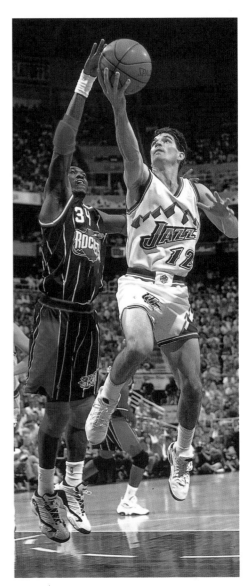

ROLL OF HONOR

Conference/Division	Western/Midwest			
First NBA year	1974–75			
Home Arena details	Delta Center (built 1991, capacity 19,911)			
Former cities/nicknames	New Orleans Jazz (1974–79)			
NBA Championships	None			

Playing Record	G	W	L	Pct
Regular Season	1968	1043	925	.530
Playoffs (Series 16–15)	157	81	76	.516

enough to keep the franchise from moving west. It wasn't until Frank Layden assumed control in 1981 that the Jazz started making some noise, and in 1983–84, the team reached the playoffs for the first time.

With virtually total control of the roster, Layden went to work molding exactly the kind of team he wanted. Starting with a nucleus that included Adrian Dantley, Darrell Griffith and Danny Schayes, Layden pushed and pulled the team to its first winning season. By 1984, he had added Thurl Bailey and 7–4 Mark Eaton, who had been discovered by a UCLA assistant coach while working as an automobile mechanic.

With a Midwest Division title also coming that season, the Jazz had arrived. Staying among the elite, however, proved difficult until Utah made the two most important draft choices in franchise history.

The Jazz used a first-round pick to select point guard John Stockton in 1984 and a year later used another for 6–9 forward Karl Malone.

Since Malone arrived, Utah have not had a losing season.

Indeed, Malone and Stockton have developed into an ideal inside-outside combination. Although the Jazz have operated without a top-flight center, Malone has held Utah together under the basket. Out front, Stockton has developed into the greatest assist man in league history, passing Magic Johnson in total career assists in 1995. Stockton's passes, fundamentally sound and almost always on the mark, have helped Malone become one of the highest scoring power forwards ever.

With the team up and running, Layden turned over the coaching duties to former Bulls star Jerry Sloan. With Hornecek arriving midway through the 1993–94 season, the Jazz added yet another veteran scorer to the starting lineup. They reached the Western Conference Finals in 1994 and won a team-record 60 games in 1995.

The Jazz finally broke through the Western Conference logjam in the 1996–97 season. Malone had a dominant season, edging Michael Jordan for MVP honors, and the Jazz stormed to the NBA Finals. Utah won a pair of games at the Delta Center to tie the series at 2–2, but Chicago was able to rally and win the NBA Championship.

The 1997–98 season was a repeat performance by the seasoned Utah squad. The Jazz muscled their way back to the NBA Finals, using home court advantage to win the series' first game. But once again the Bulls were able to prevail in six games. With the seemingly ageless Malone and Stockton at the helm, the Jazz remain a threat to bring an NBA Championship to Salt Lake City.

Karl Malone: The 1996–97 regular season MVP led Utah to the NBA Finals in 1997 and 1998.

JERRY SLOAN
Master Jazzman

Ask about the crooked nose and Jerry Sloan will tell you he can't remember how many times it was broken.

"I think I broke it about seven or eight times," he says with a shrug.

Sloan made up for limited skills with determination and grit. Though just 6–5 and 200 pounds, Sloan feared no one. He directed the Bulls' defense like a general directing an army and refused to give an inch, even in practice.

He made the NBA All-Defensive First Team four times and led Chicago to a string of 50-win seasons in the early 1970s. A two-time All-Star, Sloan retired in 1975 and became a coach.

When Sloan moved into the head job with the Jazz, the team responded immediately, averaging more than 50 victories a season in his first five full seasons. The Jazz also won two Midwest Division titles and 25 playoff games.

Other than Sloan's nose, there's no longer anything out of line in Utah.

Grizzlies Bear a Tough Start

Head coach Brian Winters played with former NBA star center Bob Lanier and general manager Stu Jackson once coached the New York Knicks' Patrick Ewing. So it only made sense that the Grizzlies would build their first roster around a highly skilled big man. And that's exactly what Vancouver did when it made Bryant "Big Country" Reeves the team's first No. 1 draft pick.

Long before Stu Jackson became general manager of the expansion Vancouver Grizzlies he knew the job would have as much to do with education as building a franchise from the ground up.

Vancouver's sporting landscape has been dominated by hockey from its junior ranks to the professional level. But Jackson, who coached the New York Knicks in 1989–90, thinks that's why the Grizzlies' popularity will explode once the NBA game arrives.

"That void could get filled here quickly," says Jackson, who believes in making the team and front office accessible to fans and media. "We have an opportunity, over the long term, to make the Grizzlies a focal point of conversations. My dream is that I'll be around here for 10 or 15 years, where I can actually hear and see that. Hockey here is what has been and will always be. But it's not true with this younger generation. The potential is there for a basketball explosion."

Shareef Abdur-Rahim finishes off the break.

To that end, Jackson's long-term vision can be seen in the building blocks he has used to create the Grizzlies foundation. By naming Winters, 43, as the team's first coach, Jackson chose an individual known for his ability to communicate with players. A former NBA All-Star player, Winters learned coaching as an assistant under Lenny Wilkens, who has more professional coaching victories than anyone in NBA history.

"I guess one of the greatest things I've taken from him isn't even on the basketball side," says Winters, an NBA head coach for the first time. "I think as good a basketball coach as he is, Lenny is a better man. He always had his teams ready to play. As for my own style, I'd like to think I'm a teacher."

Out on the court, Jackson started building the Grizzlies' roster with a combination of inside and outside toughness. In the expansion draft, Vancouver chose seasoned scorers Byron Scott, Gerald Wilkens and Blue Edwards to shore up the perimeter. Jackson then used additional expansion picks to add centers Antonio Harvey and Benoit Benjamin along with power forwards Kenny Gattison and Larry Stewart. Rodney Dent, Reggie Slater and Doug Edwards were also among the first Grizzlies. But it was the acquisition of former Knicks point guard Greg Anthony with Vancouver's first pick that made the day for Jackson and Winters.

The Grizzlies' front office felt the same way only a few days later when the 1995 NBA Draft produced 7–0 center Bryant "Big Country" Reeves and 6–5 shooting guard Lawrence Moten. Reeves, who starred at Oklahoma State, was the No. 6 choice overall and the first ever for the Grizzlies.

"Our decision to draft Bryant as our first-ever college pick reflects the premium we've placed on a big center," says Jackson.

ROLL OF HONOR

Conference/Division	Western/Midwest			
First NBA year	1995–96			
Home Arena details	(General Motors Place (built 1995, capacity 20,004)			
Former cities/nicknames	None			
NBA Championships	None			
Playing Record	G	W	L	Pct
Regular Season	246	48	198	.195
Playoffs	yet to qualify			

"Bryant gives us size, excellent shooting skills, solid passing, soft hands and perhaps the most important, a yeoman's work ethic."

The Grizzlies fared worse in their second season, managing just 14 wins. But another piece of the puzzle was added in the form of 6–10 forward Shareef Abdur-Rahim, who added athleticism and talent to the roster.

Winters was replaced by former Orlando coach Brian Hill, and the Grizzlies responded with their best season yet in 1997–98 as Abdur-Rahim developed into a bona fide star. The 1998 NBA Draft brought them Mike Bibby, the best point guard prospect to enter the league in years. With Bibby, the son of former NBA star Henry Bibby, running the offense, the Grizzlies are set to claw their way out of the NBA cellar.

From a Distance: Bryant Reeves shoots.

BRYANT REEVES
Big Country Arrives in B.C.

Bryant Reeves is the first to admit that the thought of an NBA career wasn't even the stuff of dreams just four years ago. As an oversized but awkward country kid from Gans, Oklahoma, a small town with just over 250 people, Reeves wasn't even sure he'd have a college career much less a professional one.

"When I started college there is no way I could have even dreamed of being taken with the sixth pick in the NBA Draft," says Reeves. "It just wasn't a realistic dream for me."

But Reeves, now a 7-foot, 292-pound center, spent countless hours developing basketball skills to match his size. He worked just as tirelessly in the weight room and by the end of his sophomore season had become the first player since Wilt Chamberlain to lead the Big Eight conference in scoring and rebounding.

In his first NBA season, Reeves showed he belonged among the league's big men. Vancouver fans fell in love with their flat-topped center, and he responded by averaging 13.3 points and 7.4 rebounds.

"The guy's a miracle," says Oklahoma State coach Eddie Sutton.

Not even Reeves would argue with that.

Hoping for a Good Spell

Former Coach Wes Unseld was the last link to a glorious past as Washington spent years trying to reload for another attack on the Eastern Conference powers. But the rebuilding process didn't get moving for good until Washington found Juwan Howard in the 1994 Draft and then traded for superstar Mitch Richmond. Suddenly the Wizards are on their way back.

One way or another Chicago has often played a key role in the success of the Washington Wizards.

The franchise originated in 1961, in what the NBA brass felt was a perfect market. Chicago had spawned the Harlem Globetrotters and some of the best college basketball of the era. But the Chicago Packers didn't capture the hearts of locals. A year later the franchise changed its name to the Zephyrs, but the impact, on and off the court, was minimal. Though stars such as Walt Bellamy and Terry Dischinger provided a solid foundation, the team was a financial disaster and, after two years, moved to Baltimore, where there was yet another nickname, this time the Bullets.

The new location did little to improve performances until 1968. With Earl "the Pearl" Monroe operating on the outside and 245-pound center Wes Unseld taking care of things under the basket, Baltimore

Juwan Howard makes the right moves.

won 57 games. Unseld was named Rookie of the Year and Most Valuable Player in 1969 after averaging 18.2 rebounds a game.

Two years later, the Bullets reached the NBA Finals for the first time, but quickly

lost to the Milwaukee Bucks. Former Boston Celtics great K.C. Jones took over the coaching duties and he led the team into the 1975 NBA Finals.

Now known as the Washington Bullets, following their move from Baltimore, the team won a franchise-record 60 regular-season games. With Unseld, Elvin Hayes, Phil Chenier and Mike Riordan, the Bullets knocked off Boston in the Eastern Conference Finals and met Golden State.

But Golden State made quick work of Washington, winning the title in four straight games. Jones lasted one more season until management returned to Chicago for its next savior. Coach Dick Motta had turned a young Chicago Bulls franchise into an Eastern Conference power.

In 1978, the Bullets returned to the NBA Finals, and this time there was only joy. With Hayes, Bobby Dandridge, Mitch Kupchak and Unseld, Washington had one of the most rugged frontlines in the league. The Bullets breezed through the first three rounds of the playoffs and beat Seattle in seven games for the NBA title.

Though the Bullets had a league best 54–28 record in 1978–79, the championship rematch went to the SuperSonics. That loss ended an era as Motta moved on a year later and the team faded with Unseld's retirement and Hayes' trade.

The franchise began a resurgence in the mid-1990s. After drafting Juwan Howard with the fifth overall pick in the 1994 NBA Draft, then trading for his college teammate, Chris Webber, five months later. The

ROLL OF HONOR	
Conference/Division	Eastern/Atlantic
First NBA year	1961–62
Home Arena details	MCI Arena (built 1997, capacity 20,500)
Former cities/nicknames	Chicago Packers (1961–62), Chicago Zephyrs (1962–63), Baltimore Bullets (1963–73), Capital Bullets (1973–74), Washington Bullets (1974–1997)
NBA Championships	1978

Playing Record	G	W	L	Pct
Regular Season	2859	1354	1505	.474
Playoffs (Series 13–20)	166	69	97	.416

★ ★ ★ ★ ★ ★ ★ ★ ★ ★

JUWAN HOWARD
Higher Education

One of the NBA's biggest messages for youngsters is to say in school and get an education. Juwan Howard has provided kids with an excellent example—his own experience.

Howard left the University of Michigan after his junior year to join the Wizards. But he kept a promise to his grandmother and graduated after taking classes throughout his rookie year.

This sort of dedication and determination is also a hallmark of Howard's on-court demeanor. At 6–9, he can score inside or outside and is a strong rebounder and passer. He earned an NBA All-Star Game berth in just his second season.

That's why the Wizards are hoping Howard can lead the team into the NBA Finals. That's what he sees in his crystal ball.

"In 10 years I hope we've won two or three NBA Championships," Howard says. "I'll be getting ready to retire and passing on the torch to the younger players coming into the NBA."

two 6–10 frontcourters were a perfect combination, and their play rubbed off on their teammates. With 7–7 Romanian center Gheorghe Muresan and point guard Rod Strickland, Washington returned to the playoffs in the 1996–97 season but the Bulls quickly swept them.

The 1997–98 season provided a new beginning for the team, as it was renamed the Wizards. But the team couldn't conjure up a playoff berth, so Webber was traded for veteran stars Mitch Richmond and Otis Thorpe.

In Howard and Richmond, the Wizards now have a potent inside-outside combination. Add in slashing swingman Calbert Cheaney as well as underrated point guard Rod Strickland, and coach Bernie Bickerstaff may have a potion powerful enough to cast a playoff spell on Washington fans.

The Washington Wizards' Calbert Cheaney tries to do some magic with a basketball.

THE PLAYOFFS

The NBA's Second Season

For six months 29 teams battle each other for 16 precious playoff spots. The best teams jockey for home-court advantage while the up-and-coming fight each other for one of the last playoff openings. As the 82-game schedule moves toward conclusion in late April, the games become more important and the skirmishes more fierce. When it's over, eight teams from each conference embark on a second season defined by its intensity and celebrated for its opportunity. After a two-month process of elimination, only the strongest is left standing.

The goal never changes. By the time the first ball is tossed into the air in the first game of every season, NBA players and coaches already have looked down the road. For most teams, success is measured by the playoffs.

"Nothing else matters," says Chicago Bulls forward Scottie Pippen. "You can get all kinds of individual honors during the regular season, but when it comes to real accomplishment, that happens in the playoffs. That's the way it's always been for this team and I'm sure that's the way it's always been for teams that win championships."

During the 82-game war that is the regular season, teams fight each other for playoff position. For some teams, merely becoming one of the 16 teams that qualify for the postseason tournament is enough. For others, getting home-court advantage and going on to the championship round is the sole measure of success. And for a few teams like Chicago, New York and Phoenix, anything short of an NBA title represents failure.

"When I was playing, we played for championships," says former Boston Celtics guard K.C. Jones. "That's all we thought about. We knew we'd make the playoffs. We were looking at another title."

HOW THE SYSTEM WORKS

The process, though rather long, is relatively simple. The eight teams each from the Western and Eastern Conferences with the best overall records in the regular season qualify for the playoffs. Regular season champions from the four divisions—Midwest, Pacific, Central and Atlantic— become the top two seeds in each conference.

The team with the best record in each conference is assured of home-court advantage through the Conference Finals. The team with the best record in the league is guaranteed home-court advantage throughout the entire playoffs.

"Home-court advantage wasn't that important to us," recalled Chicago Bulls star Michael Jordan, the first and possibly only ever five-time Finals MVP. "But for some teams that was the only way they had a chance. Winning playoff games on the road is one of the hardest things to do as a team.

"Don't get me wrong. We wanted home-court advantage. Although we learned how to win on the road, we were just like every other team. We wanted to play as much as possible."

The eight teams from each conference are seeded according to their regular-season record and division finish. There are four First Round best-of-five playoff series in each conference with the No. 1 team playing the No. 8 team, the No. 2 team meeting the No. 7 team and so on.

The winners of the First Round move into the Conference Semifinals. The big change is that the series becomes best-of-seven. Once again, the team with the best regular-season record has home-court advantage, or four of the seven games on its floor.

The site of the series goes back and forth in a 2–2–1–1–1 format. In other words, the first two games are played in one city followed by two games in the other. After that the teams alternate until a winner is determined. The Conference Finals are set up the same way as the Conference Semifinals.

The format changes only slightly in the NBA Finals, where the Western Conference champion meets the Eastern Conference champ. Again, the team with the best regular-season record gets home-court advantage in the seven-game series. But this time, the series is set up in a 2–3–2 format, a change that was instituted in 1985 to lessen the burden of travel on the participants.

1994

New York vs. Houston

Patrick Ewing and Hakeem Olajuwon had spent nearly a decade lifting their respective franchises toward greatness. But Olajuwon had failed in his only previous trip to the NBA Finals, while Ewing had never even had the opportunity. All that changed when they lined up opposite one another in the 1994 Finals.

GAME	1994 NBA FINALS		
1	Houston	85–78	New York
2	New York	91–83	Houston
3	Houston	93–89	New York
4	New York	91–82	Houston
5	New York	91–84	Houston
6	Houston	86–84	New York
7	Houston	90–84	New York

They had come from different parts of the world but, in June 1994, they occupied the center of professional basketball.

Patrick Ewing, born in Jamaica and raised near Boston, and Hakeem Olajuwon, the Nigerian who came to the United States to become a basketball player, became two of the most dominant big men to ever play the game. Their size, speed and remarkable quickness were always matched by fierce competitive streaks. Since they arrived in New York and Houston respectively, the twice-yearly battles between Ewing and Olajuwon had almost always been special.

By the time they lined up for Game 7 of the 1994 NBA Finals, the war between the Knicks and Rockets had exacted a toll on both of them. Ewing, playing on sore knees, had been unable to find his shooting touch. In an 86–84 loss to Houston in Game 6, Ewing had hit just 6-of-20 shots in 45 grueling minutes.

"I don't care what I shoot," said Ewing, "as long as we win."

Though Olajuwon appeared fresher and at times too quick for Ewing at the offensive end, the Knicks surged behind relentless defensive pressure. The NBA's No. 1 defensive team during the regular season, New York carved out a 91–84 victory in Game 5. As the series returned to Houston, the Knicks were only a game away from their first title in 21 years.

But as it turned out, New York was close and nothing more. In Houston, the series turned toward Olajuwon. With less than 40 seconds left in Game 6, Olajuwon stole a pass and partially blocked a John Starks shot to secure Houston's slim victory and tie the series.

In Game 7, history sided with Olajuwon. The home team had won the past 19 times a playoff series had gone to Game 7, a string going back to the 1982 Eastern Conference Finals.

"I think playing for the championship transcends any history in the playoffs," insisted Riley.

History was one thing, Olajuwon, however, was quite another. Playing 46 minutes in Game 7, Olajuwon lifted the Rockets and carried them to a 90–84 victory and the franchise's first NBA Championship.

Battle of the Titans: New York's Patrick Ewing (33) hooks over Finals MVP Hakeem Olajuwon.

1995
Houston vs. Orlando

The NBA Finals once again became a battle of two big men—Houston's Hakeem Olajuwon and Orlando's Shaquille O'Neal. Not since Bill Russell and Wilt Chamberlain squared off in the 1960s had two centers of such star power matched up for the NBA title.

GAME	1995 NBA FINALS		
1	Houston	120–118	Orlando
2	Houston	117–106	Orlando
3	Houston	106–103	Orlando
4	Houston	113–101	Orlando

Hakeem the Dream had led his Rockets to the 1994 NBA Championship, but many experts expected Orlando's Shaq Attack to overcome Houston's edge in experience. The Magic had the homecourt advantage and expected to get off to a fast start behind O'Neal, point guard Anfernee Hardaway and power forward Horace Grant.

However, Houston remembered that earlier in the postseason, the Magic had won the first playoff game in the franchise's history. Using experience gained in the previous year's championship run, the Rockets overcame a 20-point deficit to send Game 1 into overtime. Olajuwon tipped in a Clyde Drexler miss with just a fraction of a second left on the clock in overtime to take a 1–0 advantage.

The Rockets weren't satisfied with stealing one game on Orlando's home court. Proving that the Rockets' firepower extended beyond Olajuwon, Houston got a 31-point performance from backup guard Sam Cassell in Game 2 en route to a 117–106 victory.

The scene shifted to Houston for Games 3 and 4, but the outcome was all to familiar to the Magic. Orlando could not pound the ball inside to O'Neal often enough down the stretch of Game 3, and forward Robert Horry sank a clutch three-pointer to seal the win for Houston, 106–103.

The Magic did not give up in Game 4, but the Rockets

were simply too much. Their 113–101 win sealed the sweep and gave Houston a second straight title. It was the first NBA Championship in Drexler's career. As a member of the Portland Trail Blazers, Clyde the Glide had lost in two previous NBA Finals appearances.

And what of the O'Neal–Olajuwon battle in the pivot? O'Neal had a great series, averaging 28 points and 12.5 rebounds. But the crafty veteran Olajuwon outdid his younger foe, averaging 32.8 points and 11.5 rebounds while claiming his second consecutive NBA Finals MVP award.

Head to Head: Hakeem and Shaq head up in game 1.

1996

Chicago vs. Seattle

For just the 15th time in NBA history, the 1996 NBA Finals featured a show-down between the No. 1 and No. 2 teams in the league. Chicago, which had stormed to a record-setting 72–10 record in the regular season, was the league's top team. Seattle earned the No. 2 distinction with a 64–18.

Out to Win: Michael Jordan and Dennis Rodman.

In the previous 14 No. 1–No. 2 matchups, the No. 1 team had won 11 times. The SuperSonics, fresh off back-to-back first-round playoff exits in the past two seasons, wanted to prove that they were as good as their gaudy regular-season records. Power forward Shawn Kemp and point guard Gary Payton were among the best in the league, but the Sonics and coach George Karl had little postseason success to show for it.

Meanwhile, it appeared a mere formality that Michael Jordan's Bulls would claim the title based on their amazing regular season. Once the postseason began, Jordan and forwards Scottie Pippen and Dennis Rodman sparked Chicago to an 11–1 record in the Eastern Conference playoffs.

The Bulls kept on charging as the 1996 NBA Finals started. Before the Sonics knew what had hit them, the Bulls had taken a 3–0 lead in the series behind Jordan's clutch shooting and Rodman's dominance on the boards. Kemp was a one-man show for the Sonics, but he couldn't win games by himself.

On the verge of elimination, Seattle fought back with its trademark defense, which stifled the Bulls in Games 4 and 5. The series headed back to Chicago, where the Sonics felt they had a chance to come all the way back from the 3–0 deficit.

It wasn't to be. Coach Phil Jackson motivated his Chicago troops to deliver a knockout performance on the defensive end of the court. When the buzzer sounded at the end of Game 6, the Bulls had an 87–75 victory and a fourth NBA Championship in six years.

Including the regular season and the playoffs, the Bulls had compiled an amazing 87–13 record during the 1995–96 season. After the game, Jordan—who was the MVP of the 1996 All-Star Game, regular season and NBA Finals—collapsed to the floor with relief and jubilation. After more than a year away from basketball, he had come back as a winner.

"I had a lot of things on my heart and on my mind," said Jordan, who dedicated the Game 6 win on Father's Day to his late father. "I think deep down my heart was geared to what was important to me, which is my family."

The decisive victory capped a dream season for Chicago. Aside from Jordan's impressive slew of MVP awards, the Bulls were a well-rounded team with many weapons. Jordan, Pippen and Rodman were all named to the All-Defense first team. Jackson was recognized as the NBA's Coach of the Year. For the Sonics, the loss didn't diminish their season's accomplishments. But in the end, the Bulls left no doubt as to who the NBA's No. 1 team was.

GAME	1996 NBA FINALS		
1	Chicago	107–90	Seattle
2	Chicago	92–88	Seattle
3	Chicago	108–86	Seattle
4	Seattle	107–86	Chicago
5	Seattle	89–78	Chicago
6	Chicago	87–75	Seattle

1997

Chicago vs. Utah

The Chicago Bulls came into the 1997 NBA Finals with one of the best-known duos in basketball history: Michael Jordan and Scottie Pippen. Their opponents, however, featured another potent one-two punch. Utah had Karl Malone and John Stockton.

Utah's two superstars hoped they could steal a championship from the heavily favored Bulls as the series got underway in Chicago. The raucous fans in the United Center expected their beloved Bulls to pummel the challengers, but the game was a back-and-forth affair. The final three-and-a-half minutes were especially breathtaking, as the lead changed hands six times before the game came down to a superstar showdown. With the game tied at 82 and just 9.2 seconds left in the game, Malone missed two free throws. The Bulls got the ball back and gave it to Jordan, who swished a 20-foot jumper as time expired to give the Bulls an 84–82 victory.

Game 2 was hardly a nail-biter. Jordan put on a command performance—and nearly a triple-double, with 38 points, 13 rebounds and nine assists—as the Bulls cruised to a 97–85 win. Jordan appeared to be exacting revenge from Malone for winning the regular season MVP award. After just two games, the Jazz were backed into a corner.

Utah's players hardly looked intimdated as the action shifted to Salt Lake City's Delta Center for Game 3. The Jazz came out smoking on their home court, as Malone shifted back into MVP gear. He scored 22 points in the first half and 37 for the game as Utah raced to a 104–93 victory.

Game 4 was almost identical to Game 1. After another hard-fought battle, the outcome came down to Malone on the foul

Michael Jordan wins "one for the thumb."

line and Jordan taking a key shot. This time, the results were different. Jordan had a chance to put the Bulls ahead by three

points with less than a minute to play but missed a jumper. Stockton snared the rebound, and launched a daring pass to Malone. It was perfect; Malone made the layup to give the Jazz a lead they would not lose. He later sank a free throw to pad the Jazz's lead and sealed the game, 78–73, to even the NBA Finals at two games each.

The Jazz had one more home game, and Utah fans were hopeful their team could take a 3–2 lead back to Chicago. Bulls fans had reason to be pessimistic when they learned that Jordan was unwell. Jordan was sick to his stomach prior to the game, but he spent the rest of the contest making Utah queasy. In one of the most heroic NBA Finals performances ever, Jordan tossed in 38 points. Chicago won, 90–88, and took a 3–2 Finals lead.

Jordan said: "I was really tired and very weak. At halftime I told [coach] Phil [Jackson] to use me in spurts. I almost played myself into passing out. I came in and I was almost dehydrated and it was all just to win a basketball game."

The NBA Finals returned to Chicago for Game 6 and Jordan returned to health, both of which were bad news for the Jazz. As with Game 1, the Utah crew refused to roll over and play dead in front of the Bulls' fans. The Jazz held the lead in the fourth quarter, but Chicago summoned yet another comeback. With the game tied 86–86 in the last seconds, the Bulls called a timeout. Jackson drew up a play for Jordan, who passed on advice to backup guard Steve Kerr.

Kerr recalled: "He [Jordan] said, 'You be ready, Stockton is going to come off you.' I said, 'I'll be ready, I'll knock it down.'"

The scene unfolded just as Jordan predicted. He hit Kerr with a pass at the top of the key, and Kerr drilled it to give the Bulls the lead. Pippen stole the ball as Utah tried one last shot and Toni Kukoc dunked at the buzzer to give Chicago a 90–86 victory and the 1997 NBA Championship.

GAME	1997 NBA FINALS		
1	Chicago	84–82	Utah
2	Chicago	97–85	Utah
3	Utah	104–93	Chicago
4	Utah	78–73	Chicago
5	Chicago	90–88	Utah
6	Chicago	90–86	Utah

1998

Chicago vs. Utah

• •

Like all great prize fights, the Bulls–Jazz showdown of 1997 deserved a rematch. The bout unfolded differently the second time around, but in the end Chicago remained the undisputed champion.

• •

In 1997, the Bulls had opened the series with a quick one-two combination of wins on their home floor. But 1998 saw the first two games of the NBA Finals contested on Utah's home court, the Delta Center.

The Jazz, benefitting from 10 days off prior to the Finals after sweeping the Lakers in the Western Conference Finals, were able to stagger the Bulls — seventh-game winners over the Pacers — with an opening 88–85 overtime victory. Chicago's star duo, Michael Jordan and Scottie Pippen, looked winded, while the Jazz combo of Karl Malone and John Stockton looked ready to add an NBA Championship to their resumes. Stockton led the way with 25 points, and NBA observers wondered if the Bulls had enough fuel left in their tanks for another arduous series.

Chicago replied with a 93–88 victory in Game 2, but it was hardly a work of art. Jordan scored 37 points, but needed 33 shots to do so. Malone was off his game as well, failing to score a basket in the second half. With the two teams' leading scorers in a funk, other players rose to the occasion. Pippen notched 21 points, while Jeff Hornacek added 20 for the Jazz.

When the series moved to Chicago for Game 3, most expected a hard-fought game. And they were wrong. From the start, the Bulls outshot, outrebounded, outhustled and outplayed the Jazz at every turn. When the dust settled, the Bulls had delivered a potential knockout punch with a resounding 96–54 win. The Jazz, despite a resurgent performance from Malone,

mustered only 23 points in the second half and set a new low for points in a game since the NBA instituted the 24-second shot clock. The Bulls had the game all but wrapped up by halftime, and fans had to wonder if they had the NBA Finals wrapped up as well.

The Bulls put the Jazz on the ropes with another win in Game 4, this time 86–82. Surprisingly, Chicago's star offensive performer down the stretch was rebounding dynamo Dennis Rodman. The veteran forward hit four free throws to put the Bulls in position to clinch the title at home, the last game to be played in Chicago.

The Jazz, while staggered, refused to go down for the count in the Windy City. Game 5 was Malone's time to shine, and he dominated the game with 39 points and a key basket late in the fourth quarter. Despite the Mailman's heroics, the Bulls nearly won the game with a last-ditch push. A long three-point attempt by Jordan at the buzzer would have won the series for Chicago had it not barely missed.

Utah carried the momentum back to the Delta Center for Game 6, which was a toe-to-toe slugfest from the start. Malone continued to play like a man possessed, but Jordan literally took over the game in the final minute. The Bulls trailed 86–83 when Jordan knifed through the Jazz defense for a basket. On defense, he stripped the ball from Malone on a brilliant play, then hit a jumper to give the Bulls the lead with 5.2 seconds to play. Jordan finished with 45 points, and when Stockton's desperation three-pointer fell away from the rim, the Bulls had clinched the 87–86 victory that gave Chicago its sixth NBA Championship in eight seasons.

Michael Jordan: six-time NBA Playoffs MVP.

GAME	1998 NBA FINALS		
1	Utah	88–85	Chicago
2	Chicago	93–88	Utah
3	Chicago	96–54	Utah
4	Chicago	86–82	Utah
5	Utah	83–81	Chicago
6	Chicago	87–86	Utah

SUPERSTARS OF THE NBA

They have turned the NBA into one of the greatest shows on and off Earth by combining speed, strength, style and substance. And the brightest of them are known as Superstars.

The game has always revolved around its greatest players, constantly evolving with each new talent and turning on the brilliance of each era's stars. In the early days, George Mikan dominated with a rare combination of size and skill. It was Mikan who set the stage for later star centers such as Bill Russell, Wilt Chamberlain and Kareem Abdul-Jabbar by dominating at both ends of the court.

So gifted were the early giants that rules were actually changed to keep them from twisting the entire game toward themselves. The introduction of the 24-second clock to limit offensive possession time and thus speed up the game opened the floor to another group of players. All-around stars such as Oscar Robertson showed how smaller players with multiple talents could dominate just as much as the era's big men.

But then the game took off for good on the wings of players such as Julius "Dr. J" Erving. His high-flying style and all-around brilliance created a whole new level. Dominique Wilkins, Hakeem Olajuwon, Patrick Ewing, David Robinson, and Michael Jordan, players who combined size, speed and remarkable leaping ability, became some of the game's greatest scorers. Others such as Magic Johnson and Larry Bird, with near-perfect fundamentals and an innate understanding of the game, lifted the NBA game into one of the most popular team sports in the world.

LEFT: Air Jordan in mid-flight against the New York Knicks.
RIGHT: Anfernee "Penny" Hardaway tries to find a way around Hakeem "The Dream" Olajuwon.

CHARLES BARKLEY

They Call Him Sir Charles

Charles Barkley didn't look like a basketball player as a boy growing up in tiny Leeds, Alabama. His legs were heavy, his body short and wide. Coaches didn't think he was tall enough to play inside or fast enough to play guard.

So Charles went to work. He spent hours jumping back and forth over the fence behind his family's small house. By the time he entered Auburn University, his huge frame was supported by equally strong legs. Soon, nobody cared about Barkley's relatively short stature. The Philadelphia 76ers, then one of the league's top teams with Moses Malone and Julius Erving, made Barkley the No. 5 pick in the 1984 NBA Draft.

Almost immediately Barkley, who was nicknamed "The Round Mound of Rebound," proved to be an even better player in the NBA. With the game played more freely, Barkley used his strength and speed to punish players a half-foot taller. He used his bulk to hold his ground under the basket for rebounds and his lightning quick jumping ability to go up and over taller opponents.

But he could also score from anywhere on the court. In his first nine

Call Me Sir: Charles Barkley sails in for another score.

CAREER RECORD

PERSONAL											
Birthplace/Date	Leeds, Alabama/2.20.63										
Height /Weight	6–6/252										
AWARDS											
MVP	1993										
All-Star Selection	1987–98 (did not play 1994, 1997)										
Finals MVP	None										
CAREER											
University	Auburn (1981–84)										
Pro. Career	14 seasons, Philadelphia 76ers (1984–92), Phoenix Suns (1992–96), Houston Rockets (1996–98)										

PLAYING RECORD	G	FG	Pct	FT	Pct	Reb	Ast	Stl	Bl	Pts	ppg
Regular Season	1011	8089	.544	6086	.736	11821	3960	1591	871	22792	22.5
Playoffs	119	973	.513	731	.718	1527	467	187	106	2739	23.0
All-Star	9	45	.495	20	.625	60	16	12	4	113	12.6

The Round Mound of Rebound: Barkley lives up to his nickname as he snares another board.

NBA seasons, he never shot less than 52 percent from the floor. Barkley could hit short jump shots, long three-pointers and slam as well as any player in history.

"With the Sixers, even when he was new, Charles got us awake at times," says former Philadelphia guard Maurice Cheeks. "Sometimes we got on too low a flame, but then Charles would come along and slam the ball or something and we'd remember what we were out there for. And we had better know because you didn't want Charles mad at you."

Barkley, who became known as "Sir Charles," became a fixture in the NBA All-Star Game and one of the most popular—and controversial—players in the league. Despite his years of greatness in Philly, he was unable to lead the Sixers to an NBA title. In search of that elusive goal, Barkley was traded to Phoenix in a blockbuster trade in 1992. Charles was the leading scorer on the original Dream Team that won a gold medal for the U.S. at the 1992 Olympics, then led the Suns to the NBA Finals in 1993, the year he was named

league MVP. The Suns lost to the Chicago Bulls and Barkley's buddy, Michael Jordan, but Barkley's status as one of the game's great players was cemented.

1996 saw Charles—named one of the NBA's 50 Greatest Players—change teams again, this time moving to the Houston Rockets. During the season, Charles became the fourth player in NBA history to tally 20,000 points, 10,000 rebounds and 3,500 assists, joining Hall of Famers Wilt Chamberlain, Kareem Abdul-Jabbar and Elgin Baylor. Despite nagging injuries, Barkley helped the Rockets to reach the 1997 Western Conference Finals. He continues to be an elite player despite recurring injuries that have forced him to start some games on the bench rather than on the floor. Barkley remains focused on filling just about the only gap in his resume: an NBA Championship.

> ●●●●●●●●●●●●●●●●●●●●●●●●●
> ## "CHARLES IS A TOTALLY DOMINANT PLAYER. GUYS WHO ARE 6–4 OR 6–5 JUST AREN'T SUPPOSED TO BE ABLE TO DO THAT IN THE NBA."
> **Larry Bird**
> ●●●●●●●●●●●●●●●●●●●●●●●●●

PATRICK EWING

New York's Tower of Power

Quiet and soft-spoken, with a gentle smile and manner, Patrick Ewing seems nothing like the menacing shot-blocker that he is on the basketball court.

Watch Ewing long enough and it's hard to believe that he started playing basketball late in his youth. Watch him rally the New York Knicks past another opponent, or slap away a shot attempt, and it seems unlikely Ewing ever lacked confidence or consistency. Look over Ewing's resume, which includes an NCAA championship at Georgetown University and Olympic gold medals in 1984 and 1992, and it's hard to think of him of anything less than the dominant big man he has become.

"Very early on, Patrick had to learn, had to be convinced, how good he really was, how good he could be," says Georgetown coach and former NBA center John Thompson. "Defensively, to help him with both his confidence and his consistency, I told him to go up and block every shot and take his chances on being called for goal-tending. The guy on the other team would remember that."

Whatever the lesson, it worked. Ewing developed into a college star at Georgetown before graduating to the New York Knicks as the first pick in the 1985 NBA Draft. Though injuries slowed Ewing in

Patrick Ewing adds another two points.

CAREER RECORD

PERSONAL											
Birthplace/Date	Kingston, Jamaica/8.5.62										
Height /Weight	7-0/255										
AWARDS											
MVP	None										
All- Star Selections	1986, 1988–97 (did not play due to injury 1986, 1997)										
Finals MVP	None										
CAREER											
University	Georgetown (1981–85)										
Pro. Career	13 seasons, New York Knicks (1985–98)										

PLAYING RECORD	G	FG	Pct	FT	Pct	Reb	Ast	Stl	Bl	Pts	ppg
Regular Season	939	8652	.513	4756	.744	9778	1987	995	2574	22079	23.5
Playoffs	110	967	.478	497	.721	1184	259	98	271	2439	22.2
All-Star	9	44	.556	18	.692	60	7	11	16	106	11.8

Shadow Box: Ewing is still a dominating presence at both ends of the court, averaging better than 20 points and 10 rebounds per game for his career.

his first two NBA seasons, the marvelous talents were obvious to everyone, particularly opposing players.

Ewing was named NBA Rookie of the Year in 1986 despite missing 32 games that season. In the 1989–89 season he averaged 28.6 points while scoring from virtually anywhere on the court. He slammed down rim-rattling dunks, lofted soft fallaway jumpers and, when teams forced him outside, dropped long-range jump shots. He also averaged nearly 11 rebounds a game and blocked a career-high 327 shots in 82 games.

Two years later, with Pat Riley taking over on the bench, Ewing's Knicks had become one of the NBA's most devastating teams. New York, led by Ewing's relentless defensive play, took the eventual champion Chicago Bulls to the Eastern Conference Finals in 1993, narrowly missing a shot at the championship round.

Although Ewing will be 36 years old when the 1998–99 season tips off, he has hardly slowed down. His legendary work-

outs have kept him in top shape, and the Knicks have wisely built a powerful team around Ewing.

A severe right wrist injury limited Ewing to just 26 games in 1997–98, the fewest he's ever played in his NBA career. It was thought he would miss the playoffs as well, but Ewing worked hard to return for the Knicks' second-round series against the Pacers. While he was less than 100 percent, it was yet another example of Ewing showing his leadership to NBA fans.

Deep thought: Ewing is a study in concentration even when the game stops.

ANFERNEE HARDAWAY

Penny Proves his Worth

A year after Orlando used the No. 1 pick in the 1992 Draft to select Shaquille O'Neal, fate shined on the Magic once again. This time, however, Orlando used the No. 1 pick on Chris Webber but almost immediately traded him to Golden State for a 20-year-old guard called Penny.

No one was sure what to do until John Gabriel, Orlando's personnel director, decided he needed one more look at Anfernee Hardaway. In a quiet gym filled only with Magic front office staff, he put on a dazzling display of speed, quickness, stamina and leadership in a series of games with veteran players. The workout made the decision easy: with O'Neal in the middle, it was clear that Hardaway was the player the Magic needed most.

Hardaway, a lean 6–7 guard, has been even better than Gabriel hoped. While his size and point guard skills draw the comparisons to Johnson, it's Hardaway's power dunks and long-range shooting ability that make him unique. Tree Rollins, a former teammate in Orlando, remembers one slam in particular over New York's Patrick Ewing that left everyone rubbing their eyes.

"Patrick is seven feet and about 250 pounds, and Penny is 6–7 and skinny as a rail," says Rollins. "When Penny took off for the hoop, I thought Patrick would either get the block or flatten him. But Penny just explod-

Anfernee Hardaway shows his leaping ability.

CAREER RECORD

PERSONAL											
Birthplace/Date	Memphis, Tennessee/7.16.72										
Height /Weight	6–7/215										
AWARDS											
MVP	None										
All-Star Selection	1995–98										
Finals MVP	None										
CAREER											
University	Memphis (1990–93)										
Pro. Career	5 seasons, Orlando Magic (1993–98)										

PLAYING RECORD	G	FG	Pct	FT	Pct	Reb	Ast	Stl	Bl	Pts	ppg
Regular Season	319	2241	.481	1419	.773	1468	2077	607	168	6227	19.5
Playoffs	41	319	.467	189	.747	185	272	77	32	903	22.0
All-Star	4	30	.625	10	.833	15	24	4	0	55	13.8

Don't look back: Anfernee Hardaway is the 1990s prototype for the athletic guard with moves such as this to the basket.

> **"PICKING A FAVORITE PENNY HARDAWAY PLAY IS LIKE PICKING OUT WHICH ONE OF THE STARS UP IN THE SKY SHINES THE BRIGHTEST. THERE'S SO MANY OF 'EM, YOU JUST CAN'T PICK ONE."**
>
> Larry Finch, University of Memphis head coach.

special, I can feel the vibe from the crowd. I live for the *ooh*, the *aah*."

Penny truly proved his worth to Magic fans during the 1996–97 season, when O'Neal departed for the Los Angeles Lakers. Despite a knee injury, Hardaway moved his game to the center of the Orlando attack. He combined dazzling playmaking skills and explosive scoring bursts to carry the Magic into the 1997 NBA playoffs where, despite averaging 38.7 points in the last three games of a five-game series, Orlando lost to the Miami Heat, ending Penny's playoff run.

An assortment of injuries kept Hardaway out of all but 19 games in 1997–98, but he is excited about his future. The Magic may move him from point guard to shooting guard, allowing him to play more in the style of Michael Jordan. That's a truly magical opportunity for Orlando fans and Hardaway alike.

Hardaway is the Orlando playmaker too.

ed to the basket, and, *wham!* It was over."

In an often spectacular rookie season in 1993–94, Hardaway averaged 16.0 points, 6.6 assists, 5.4 rebounds and more than two steals a game. And in the playoffs he produced better numbers in virtually every category.

More importantly, the Magic improved dramatically, winning a franchise record 50 games. By the start of the 1994–95 season, Hardaway was considered the league's next great guard. Orlando had improved when O'Neal arrived, but they didn't take the next step forward until Hardaway came aboard.

In 1994–95, with the addition of former Chicago forward Horace Grant, the Magic finished with the best record in the Eastern Conference and made it all the way through to the NBA Finals, where the Houston Rockets swept Orlando. Seattle's All-Star guard Gary Payton described Hardaway in five words: "Best guard in the NBA."

Hardaway is not sure the label fits just yet. But he does admit to a fondness for the kind of plays that bring fans to their feet.

"I like to entertain," he says. "Most of all, I want to win, but when I do something

GRANT HILL
The Key to Detroit's Future

The comparisons started the moment Grant Hill threw down his first thundering dunk. With a long, slender body and enough skills to play four positions, Hill recalled some of the league's brightest stars.

The quick first step reminded some of Michael Jordan. Others saw Scottie Pippen in Hill's rare combination of talents. Indeed, Hill proved immediately he belonged amid the NBA elite on and off the court. Intelligent, cool and mature beyond his years, Hill did look a lot like Jordan during his first winter in Detroit.

The Pistons, looking for another star after Isiah Thomas retired, wanted only one player in the 1994 NBA Draft. Though they had the third pick, Detroit worked feverishly to move up.

Billy McKinney, former vice president of operations, said: "I wanted Grant Hill. We all did. But we were afraid someone else would take him before the third pick."

Nobody did. Hill, who was on back-to-back NCAA Championship teams at Duke, went to the Pistons and before he played a single NBA game, he had fielded endorsement calls from some of the world's largest corporations. However unusual his athletic gifts, Hill's personality was even more unique.

"He's a special person," said Don Chaney, the Pistons' coach in Hill's rookie season, "not only in the way he plays, but how he handles himself. His parents did a great job instilling values in him."

Grant Hill grew up in the shadow of a famous father, Calvin, who starred as an NFL runningback. Refusing to expose his son to the brutality of his profession, Calvin

Unstoppable: Grant Hill takes it down low.

Not this time: Hill shows his defensive and leaping abilities by snaring a rebound from above the rim against the Hawks.

guided Grant toward soccer. For much of his early athletic life, Grant thought that was to be his game. At least until he started to grow. Basketball eclipsed soccer, and college coaches were soon knocking at his door.

"It just seems like yesterday I was in high school," he says, "pretending I was Julius Erving and pretending I was Isiah Thomas and pretending I was Michael Jordan. Every time I stepped on the court, I was somebody else. Now, in some way I'm kind of in their shoes, in the sense that people do the same with me—I guess. So I'm told. It's just hard to believe."

These days, nothing about Hill surprises anyone but himself. He not only got off to a brilliant start in his first season, but Hill became the first rookie to ever lead the fan voting for the All-Star Game.

Hill revived the Pistons franchise, leading them to the playoffs in his second and third seasons. He was a member of the third Dream Team squad that won Olympic gold in 1996, then was named to the All-NBA first team in 1997. Hill posted 13 triple-doubles on his way to winning the 1997 IBM Award for his overall statistical contribution. He also finished in the NBA's top 20 in points, rebounds, assists, steals and minutes per game in the 1996–97 season.

Hill's stellar play continued into 1997–98. He led the NBA with four triple-doubles, increasing his career total to 28. Hill ranked in the top 15 in six different statistical categories, earning a place on the All-NBA second team as well as a fourth consecutive start in the NBA All-Star game.

As one of the game's top players, and the cornerstone of the Pistons' rebuilding plans, Hill hopes to add an NBA Championship to his list of accomplishments.

CAREER RECORD

PERSONAL

Birthplace/Date	Dallas, Texas/10.5.72
Height /Weight	6–8/225

AWARDS

MVP	None
All-Star Selection	1995–98
Finals MVP	None

CAREER

University	Duke (1990–1994)
Pro. Career	4 seasons, Detroit Pistons (1994–98)

PLAYING RECORD	G	FG	Pct	FT	Pct	Reb	Ast	Stl	Bl	Pts	ppg
Regular Season	311	2312	.471	1788	.734	2572	2035	511	211	6434	20.7
Playoffs	8	312	.472	177	.755	56	38	7	5	175	21.9
All-Star	4	22	.611	5	.500	9	12	5	1	50	12.5

"I ALWAYS FELT HE WOULD BE THE NEXT IMPACT PLAYER IN THE LEAGUE. I THINK HE'S IN A CLASS BY HIMSELF."

Former Denver VP Allan Bristow

MICHAEL JORDAN
Rare Air

According to Michael Jordan, it all started with "The Shot."

J ust a freshman at the University of North Carolina, Jordan hit the first game-winning shot of what would become an illustrious career. With the clock winding down, Jordan drained a medium-range jump shot that propelled North Carolina to the national championship and a 63–62 victory over rival Georgetown.

"That's where I think my career really began," says Jordan. "I proved to myself that I could deliver in a pressure situation."

And Jordan never stopped delivering. He led the U.S. men's basketball team to the Gold Medal in 1984 Los Angeles Olympics before starting an often amazing professional career in

Look Out Below: Air Jordan lifts off against Philadelphia.

Chicago. After leading the Bulls to three consecutive championships he stunned the basketball world in 1993 by announcing his retirement from the game.

Then, after briefly playing professional baseball in the Chicago White Sox system, Jordan returned to the NBA in 1995 with just over a month left in the regular season and led a revived Bulls team into the NBA Playoffs once again.

Jordan averaged 28.2 points while leading the team in rebounds, assists and steals and was named NBA Rookie of the Year in 1985. Ironically, it was Jordan's second season that left a lasting impression. After missing 64 regular season games with a broken foot, Jordan returned in time for the playoffs against the eventual champion Boston Celtics.

Jordan scored 49 points in Game 1 at

CAREER RECORD

PERSONAL

Birthplace/Date	Brooklyn, NY/2.17.63
Height /Weight	6–6/216

AWARDS

MVP	1988, 1991, 1992, 1996, 1998
All-Star Selections	1985–93 (did not play 1986, injured), 1996–98
Finals MVP	1991, 1992, 1993, 1996, 1997, 1998

CAREER

University	North Carolina (1981–84)
Pro. Career	13 seasons, Chicago Bulls (1984–93, 1995–98)

PLAYING RECORD	G	FG	Pct	FT	Pct	Reb	Ast	Stl	Bl	Pts	ppg
Regular Season	930	10962	.505	6798	.838	5836	5012	2306	828	29277	31.5
Playoffs	179	2188	.487	1463	.828	1152	1022	376	158	5987	33.4
All-Star	11	97	.503	37	.740	52	49	33	6	234	21.3

Boston and then, in perhaps the greatest Playoff performance of all time, bombed Celtics' defensive whiz Dennis Johnson for 63 points in Game 2. It took two overtimes before the heavily favored Celtics eventually ended the Bulls charge.

"He just flat out came down and let us know what he was going to do and for the most part, he did it," said Boston superstar Larry Bird later. "He was a completely different player from anything I've seen. He's literally on a different level."

Jordan won seven straight scoring titles, matching Wilt Chamberlain's record, and became the league's best defensive guard.

In one of the most remarkable individual seasons in league history, Jordan was named Most Valuable Player and Defensive Player of the Year while leading the league in scoring and steals during the 1987–88 season. He also won his second Nestlé Slam-Dunk Championship.

With a competitive streak that amazed even his coaches, Jordan often left his opponents stunned and fans standing in amazement. Jordan's performances were so electrifying that his popularity actually transcended the sport. Thanks to the "Air Jordan" line, Nike became the world's biggest athletic shoe company. Thanks to his personality, Jordan's endorsement deals generated as much as $30 million a year.

On the court, Jordan has twice carried Chicago to three consecutive championships. He also became the first player to be named MVP in three straight NBA Finals.

Jordan retired to take up a baseball career in 1993, then returned to the Bulls in 1995. In each of the three full seasons he played since his comeback, Chicago won the NBA Championship. In his 13-year career, the Bulls have won six titles, and Jordan has been the Finals MVP in each win — despite being double- and triple-teamed by opposing defenses. Simply put, Jordan has been the "unstoppa-Bull."

Jordan, an obvious choice as one of the NBA's 50 Greatest Players, continues to add to his legendary status every time he steps on a basketball court.

· ·

"MAYBE IT'S GOD DISGUISED AS MICHAEL JORDAN."

Larry Bird

· ·

SHAWN KEMP
From Sonic Boom to Cavalier King

Just 19 years old, Shawn Kemp hadn't played a minute of college basketball in the year since he left high school when the Seattle SuperSonics called. A brilliant player throughout his youth, Kemp's 6–10 frame was as agile and quick as those of players six inches shorter.

So when he enrolled at the University of Kentucky, his coaches thought he could develop into one of the greatest college players ever. But a dispute quickly ended Kemp's stay and suddenly he was without a team and, to some extent, a future also. He then transferred to a junior college and sat out the basketball season.

On the playgrounds, Kemp's feats were already the stuff of legends. According to a friend, Kemp once dunked so hard on an outdoor rim that "sparks flew off" as the ball blew through. NBA executives had heard these stories too.

But when Kemp entered the 1989 Draft without a single year of college basketball behind him, the skeptics shook their heads. Although Moses Malone, Darryl Dawkins and Bill Willoughby had gone from high school directly into the pros, times had changed. No player, especially one as unpolished as Kemp, could make the transition these days.

Seattle thought otherwise. The SuperSonics selected Kemp with the 17th

Cavalier approach: Cleveland's Shawn Kemp goes to the hoop.

pick overall in 1989. Kemp quickly proved the doubters wrong. He could dunk as well as any player in the league, his jumping ability was stunning for a man his size. He also blocked shots with a vengeance.

In his second NBA season, Kemp aver-

CAREER RECORD

PERSONAL	
Birthplace/Date	Elkhart, Indiana/11.26.69
Height /Weight	6-10/256
AWARDS	
MVP	None
All-Star selections	1993–98
Finals MVP	None
CAREER	
University	Trinity Junior College (did not play – left school before season)
Pro. Career	9 seasons, Seattle SuperSonics (1989–97), Cleveland Cavaliers (1997–98)

PLAYING RECORD	G	FG	Pct	FT	Pct	Reb	Ast	Stl	Bl	Pts	ppg
Regular Season	705	4190	.510	3184	.730	6723	1293	883	1049	11590	16.4
Playoffs	78	504	.502	479	.798	830	161	98	137	1490	19.1
All-Star	6	22	.458	9	.750	35	10	6	4	54	9.0

aged 15.0 points and 8.4 rebounds. He also had become the foundation for a SuperSonics team on the rise.

"The thing that Shawn has had going for him all along with his skills is his love for the game and his work ethic," says former Seattle and Boston coach K.C. Jones. "That's at the core of what is making him a great player.

"The only thing that ever really concerned me as far as his quick move into the pros was how he would react to the way that the fans react to NBA-style player. A part of you must become a performer as much as a player and you could see that he was a little slow to become accustomed to the oohs and aahs of the fans at his spectacular play."

Kemp became one of the most dynamic one-man shows in basketball with a dazzling array of dunks and slams. But he also developed into a complete player, propelling the SuperSonics into the 1993 Western Conference Finals. For Kemp, that season represented his coming out party as one of the league's developing superstars.

Kemp was a member of USA Basketball's 1994 team that won the World Championships of Basketball in Canada.

Kemp led the Sonics to the playoffs in 1996 and '97, but wanted a change of scenery. He found himself traded to Cleveland prior to the 1997–98 season, and he flourished in his new home. Surrounded by other hungry young players, Kemp became the first All-Star starter in the Cavs' history and led the team into the playoffs. The undisputed team leader of the Cleveland squad, the one-time "Manchild" has reached NBA manhood.

· ·

"SHAWN HAS THAT GREAT COMBINATION OF SKILL AND CREATIVITY. HE IS VERY SIMILAR TO THE WAY I WAS WHEN I WAS YOUNGER."

Michael Jordan

· ·

Shawn Kemp aiming to add to his impressive points total.

KARL MALONE

This Mailman Delivers

Off the court, Karl Malone doesn't look much like a professional basketball player.

During the summer he operates an 18-wheel custom-made truck that hauls a variety of products to stores throughout the West. He owns a ranch in Louisiana, usually drives a pick-up truck to Utah Jazz games and would rather wear a 10-gallon hat and cowboy boots than gold chains and Gucci loafers.

But once on the court, Malone plays like a man possessed. When he isn't operating his trucking company or overseeing his ranch, Malone spends his summers lifting weights and fine-tuning his body. And no one knows that more than opposing power forwards. Not only is Malone one of the strongest players in the league, but at 6–9 and 256 pounds, he might be one of the best conditioned athletes on the planet.

"The guy is relentless," says former NBA center Dave Corzine. "He never stops working. It's almost as if he gets stronger as the game goes on. He's a machine."

Utah drafted Malone out of Louisiana Tech University, a small school tucked deep into the Louisiana countryside. Nicknamed "The Mailman" because, according to supporters, "he always delivered," Malone went to work on his game. A poor free-throw shooter as a rookie, Malone was hitting more than 70 percent two years later. An average scorer at first, Malone became the highest scoring power forward in the NBA. A sometimes disinterested defensive player, Malone became one of

Special Delivery: Malone lifts off for another two points.

CAREER RECORD

PERSONAL

Birthplace/Date	Summerfield, Louisiana/7.24.63
Height /Weight	6–9/256

AWARDS

MVP	1997
All- Star Selections	1988–98 (did not play 1990, injured)
Finals MVP	None

CAREER

University	Louisiana Tech (1981–85)
Pro. Career	13 seasons, Utah Jazz (1985–98)

PLAYING RECORD	G	FG	Pct	FT	Pct	Reb	Ast	Stl	Bl	Pts	ppg
Regular Season	1061	10290	.528	7133	.727	11376	3499	1513	874	27782	26.2
Playoffs	137	1343	.468	1002	.732	1556	400	196	109	3691	26.9
All-Star	10	58	.558	29	.725	73	19	12	5	145	14.5

the best end-to-end players in the game.

And despite playing perhaps the toughest position in the league, Malone missed just four games his first nine seasons. That's one reason Malone has been a member of the All-NBA First Team for seven consecutive years going into the 1995–96 season. He also was a member of USA Basketball's Dream Team in 1992 and 1996 and had led the Jazz in scoring and rebounding for eight straight seasons.

At the age of 33, Malone had a career year in 1996–97. He averaged 27.4 points and 9.9 rebounds per game en route to winning his first-ever MVP award and being named a first-team member of the All-NBA team and the All-Defensive team. The Mailman even delivered the Jazz to consecutive NBA Finals, in 1997 and '98, but the Chicago Bulls prevailed in a pair of hard-fought six-game series. Even in losing, Malone showed fans why he was named one of the NBA's 50 Greatest Players.

Few players have ever done as much at both ends of the court as Malone. He hasn't averaged fewer than 25.2 points a game since his second season. Overall, Malone has averaged an astounding 26.0 points and 10.8 rebounds per game since he entered the league. Which is exactly why Malone has been a member of the Western Conference All-Star team every year since 1988.

"They don't come any tougher than Karl," says former Chicago Bull John Paxson. "He runs the court like a guard, blocks shots like a center and rebounds like no one I've ever seen. There really isn't anything he can't do, which is scary for someone as big as he is."

"There's only one way I know how to play the game," says Malone, "and that's all out. If you're not going to go at it like I do, then find someplace else to play."

"IF YOU DON'T COME READY TO PLAY, KARL WILL CHEW YOU UP AND SPIT YOU OUT,"

Former NBA center Dave Corzine

Jazz Man: As strong as any player in the league and driven to succeed, Malone takes control at both ends of the court.

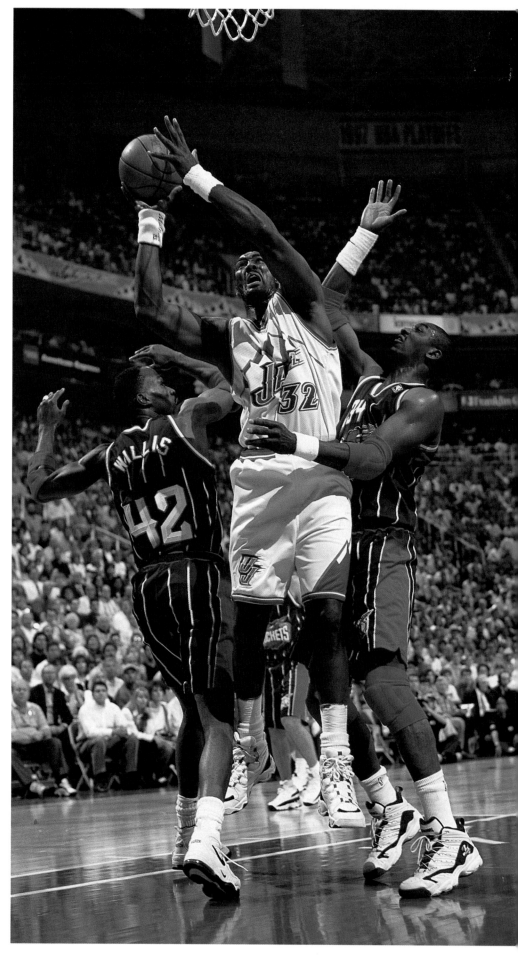

REGGIE MILLER

Long-Range Bomber

The noise never bothered Reggie Miller. He had heard the booming voices of those trying to throw off his concentration from the moment he started tossing shots toward a backyard basket.

First his brothers, then his sister, Cheryl, perhaps the most famous female basketball player ever, would hound Reggie as he attempted to compete in the often intense family basketball games. Later, as Miller grew into one of southern California's greatest high school players, opponents would chant a sarcastic "Cheryl" whenever Reggie went up for a shot.

Miller, a slender 6–7 shooting guard with remarkable range, heard all the noise but he learned not to listen. His concentration, particularly at the free throw line, became legendary. And during games, no matter how early or late, Miller's jump shot rarely faltered.

So when New York fan Spike Lee screamed at Miller during Game 5 of Indiana's 1994 Eastern Conference Finals series against the Knicks, Miller simply turned up the volume. In one of the great individual performances in playoff history, Miller bombed the Knicks for 25 fourth-quarter points and carried the Pacers to a stunning 93–86 victory at Madison Square Garden.

Reggie Miller's jump shot is one the NBA's best.

CAREER RECORD

PERSONAL	
Birthplace/Date	Riverside, California/8.24.65
Height /Weight	6–7/185
AWARDS	
MVP	None
All-Star Selection	1990, 1995, 1996, 1998
Finals MVP	None
CAREER	
University	UCLA (1983–87)
Pro. Career	11 seasons, Indiana Pacers (1987–98)

PLAYING RECORD	G	FG	Pct	FT	Pct	Reb	Ast	Stl	Bl	Pts	ppg
Regular Season	882	5695	.488	4416	.877	2788	2764	1037	220	17402	19.7
Playoffs	65	483	.469	407	.870	185	160	74	13	1530	23.5
All-Star	4	15	.536	1	.500	3	7	4	1	35	8.8

"I always had the ability to tune things out," says Miller. "And that's exactly what I did in that fourth quarter. It's almost a natural thing for me, a reflex. You have to have gone through it to get used to it. Everyone in this league knows how to play or they wouldn't be here. But the best players, guys like Michael Jordan and Larry Bird, were also great mentally. That is what it takes."

For Miller, the mental gymnastics started early. He developed his high, arching jump shots during pick up games with his brothers or one-on-one tangles with Cheryl. The form, almost from the outset, was virtually perfect.

Despite shooting primarily from the outside, Miller has been a consistently dependable scorer. He has hit 48.8 percent of his shots in the NBA, including an amazing 40.4 percent of his three-point attempts. In his first season as a Pacer, Miller broke Larry Bird's rookie record for most three-pointers. Reggie is also rock-solid from the charity stripe, hitting 87.7 percent of his free throws over his long career.

All of which is even more remarkable given Miller's early years. For most of his first five years, Miller's legs were supported by braces. Doctors warned Reggie's parents that their son might never be able to run and play like the other kids. In the Miller household, however, those kinds of negative thoughts were not accepted.

"It's all in the mind," says Miller. "That's what separates the good players from the great ones."

> "I LIKE PLAYING HARD. I'LL GIVE 110 PERCENT EVERY TIME I GO ON THE FLOOR AND I'LL DO WHATEVER IT TAKES FOR MY TEAM TO WIN."
>
> **Reggie Miller**

Untouchable: Miller (right) swerves past New York's John Starks.

ALONZO MOURNING
Seriously Hot

The scowl that routinely forms on the face of Alonzo Mourning is designed to send a message. Sensitive and caring off the court, Mourning wants teammates and opponents alike to know he's serious about taking the Heat to an NBA Championship.

At first, no one knew what to make of the furrowed brow and menacing scowl. He had been a star at Georgetown University and worked out with New York Knicks center Patrick Ewing, himself a Georgetown graduate, in the summer. Ewing's cold efficiency made an impression, but Mourning's own burning desire fueled his approach.

From the moment he arrived in Charlotte, the 6–10 center made his inten-

Alonzo Mourning warming up for the Heat.

tions clear to all those around him. Bump Mourning under the basket and he'll bump right back. It didn't matter where the loose elbow came from. Mourning never gave an inch.

"It's my intensity level on the floor," says Mourning, who played in his first All-Star Game in 1994. "People think I'm an angry player, but my expression is a different zone. I'm trying to focus what I have to do on the floor. If I played against someone who was smiling all the time, I wouldn't take him seriously. I want people

CAREER RECORD

PERSONAL											
Birthplace/Date	Chesapeake, Virgiana/2.8.70										
Height /Weight	6–10/261										
AWARDS											
MVP	None										
All Star Selection	1994–97 (did not play 1994, 1997 injured)										
Finals MVP	None										
CAREER											
University	Georgetown (1988–92)										
Pro. Career	6 seasons, Charlotte Hornets (1992–95), Miami Heat (1995–98)										
PLAYING RECORD	G	FG	Pct	FT	Pct	Reb	Ast	Stl	Bl	Pts	ppg
Regular Season	409	3009	.523	2578	.719	4117	588	269	1192	8617	21.1
Playoffs	37	248	.482	233	.670	367	51	25	103	736	19.9
All-Star	2	5	.333	2	.667	9	1	0	2	12	6.0

to take me seriously. I'm out there trying not to make a mistake, trying to work as hard as I can for my team. I can't control perceptions. But I think my game thrives off intensity."

And that's enough for the Hornets. Charlotte improved from 31 victories to 44 and the franchise's first playoff berth in Mourning's first season (1992–93). But it was during the 1993 Playoffs that Mourning proved just how much he means to the Hornets franchise and just how good he might yet become.

Mourning's often brilliant rookie season included three victories against Shaquille O'Neal's Orlando Magic. Though smaller than all of the league's premier centers, Mourning never allowed size to become an issue. Indeed, Mourning seemed to relish the role as underdog.

The 1995–96 season saw Mourning move to Miami in a blockbuster trade. Teamed with coach Pat Riley, Mourning became a dominant force for the Heat, using his determination to rally his new team to a playoff berth.

Alonzo has especially become an emotional leader during the playoffs for the Heat. Miami was on the verge of elimination against the New York Knicks in the Eastern Conference semi-finals of the 1997 NBA playoffs when Mourning took over. Matched up against his good friend Ewing, Alonzo notched 22 points, 12 rebounds, 4 blocked shots and 3 steals in the decisive seventh game to send the Heat to the Conference Finals. Mourning's Heat was cooled off by the Chicago Bulls, but 'Zo's status as one of the game's top big men was confirmed.

Miami fans have quickly become accustomed to Mourning turning up the Heat on both offense and defense.

· ·

"ALONZO'S ONE OF THE TOUGHEST GUYS IN THE LEAGUE. HE'S THE TASMANIAN DEVIL, ALL WHIRLS, TWIRLS AND TURNS."

Longtime NBA assistant coach John Bach

· ·

Mourning gets the job done, this time against the Bulls' Dennis Rodman.

HAKEEM OLAJUWON

The Dream Comes True

For most of his youth, Hakeem Olajuwon figured he'd be a soccer player. No one played basketball much in Lagos, Nigeria, while he was growing up, so he became the goalkeeper on a soccer team.

Hakeem pushes one over the Celtics.

Nowadays Olajuwon, who changed his name from Akeem to Hakeem in 1991, credits the defensive skills he learned playing soccer with helping make him a defensive giant in the NBA. Then again, the fact Olajuwon even made it to America, much less the greatest basketball league in the world, once seemed like a longshot.

He arrived at the University of Houston in 1980 with only basic basketball skills, but daunting physical gifts. Standing 7 feet tall and able to move like a smaller man, Olajuwon caught onto the game quickly thanks to summer workouts with NBA star Moses Malone.

After just three college seasons, he had become a dominant player capable of turning an entire game around almost entirely by himself.

With the No. 1 pick in the 1984 Draft, the Houston Rockets merely looked across town to find their savior. Olajuwon, who had improved dramatically during college, developed even faster in the NBA, leading the league in offensive rebounds and averaging 20.6 points and 11.9 rebounds.

Olajuwon and 7–4 Ralph Sampson became known as the "Twin Towers" and Houston became one of the league's forces. In just two seasons, the Rockets went from 29 victories and one of the league's worst records, to the 1986 NBA Finals against Larry Bird's Boston Celtics. Just as quickly, Olajuwon became a dominant center with a variety of defensive and offensive skills.

"I never felt anyone could play Hakeem one-on-one," says former NBA coach and player K.C. Jones. "To defense him you either had to deny him the ball, or bump him, and collapse players around him to force him to give up the ball."

"When he's on, which is most of the time, Hakeem is unstoppable," says Miami Heat coach Pat Riley. "We always told our defenders, 'Don't let him touch the ball.'"

By the time Olajuwon did touch the ball

CAREER RECORD

PERSONAL

Birthplace/Date	Lagos, Nigeria/1.21.63
Height /Weight	7–0/255

AWARDS

MVP	1994, 1995
All-Star selections	1985–90, 1992–97
Finals MVP	1994, 1995

CAREER

University	Houston (1980–84)
Pro. Career	14 seasons, Houston Rockets (1984–98)

PLAYING RECORD	G	FG	Pct	FT	Pct	Reb	Ast	Stl	Bl	Pts	ppg
Regular Season	1025	9706	.515	4989	.717	12199	2771	1895	3459	24422	23.8
Playoffs	136	1469	.530	732	.718	1573	454	233	465	3674	27.0
All-Star	12	45	.409	26	.520	94	17	15	23	117	9.8

Olajuwon's ball-handling skills have helped him develop into one of the best all-around centers ever to play the game.

it was usually too late to do anything but hope he missed. His spin moves to the basket often leave defenders stuck in their tracks. His ability to get into the air quickly makes him capable of dunking anything in close to the basket. But it's Olajuwon's fadeaway jump shot, like Kareem Abdul-Jabbar's sky hook, that has become the most unstoppable shot in the league.

"Hakeem is unstoppable. There's no defense anyone can devise to prevent him from doing whatever," says Magic Johnson of Olajuwon. "He controls every game he's in. He can score inside. He runs the break. He has impeccable footwork. He is the essence of a complete player." Olajuwon developed into a complete player in the course of several seasons. In the same time, he developed into a team player. He raised his assists total to get his teammates more involved. But Olajuwon is still able to take over a game and win it for the Rockets.

And it was Olajuwon who carried the Rockets to a dramatic Game 7 victory over New York in the 1994 NBA Finals for Houston's first championship.

Despite battling anemia toward the end of the 1994–95 regular season, Olajuwon led Houston not only into the playoffs but also to a second straight NBA Championship and his second personal NBA Finals MVP award, becoming only the second player—after Michael Jordan—to win the award in consecutive seasons.

Olajuwon has come a long way from his soccer days in Lagos. His astounding low-post moves have amazed fans and befuddled opponents for more than a decade now. 1996 saw "The Dream" collect an additional two honors to add to his impressive resume: After becoming a U.S. citizen, he won a gold medal on the third Dream Team, and he was named one of the NBA's 50 Greatest Players.

"IN TERMS OF RAW ATHLETIC ABILITY, HAKEEM IS THE BEST I HAVE EVER SEEN."

Magic Johnson

SHAQUILLE O'NEAL
The Shaq Attack

The stories preceded Shaquille O'Neal.

More than once during his dramatic college career at Louisiana State University, O'Neal tore a basket clean off the backboard while executing a dunk. His strength and size reminded some of Wilt Chamberlain. His ability to block shots recalled the Bill Russell era. Some wondered if O'Neal might be the best of both of them, a huge player with the athletic ability to lift an entire team.

O'Neal arrived in Orlando following the 1992 Draft, and coaches and players were still wondering just how good the 7–1, 301-pound center might become.

He was just 20 years old when the Magic played its first game with him in the middle. And no one, not even veteran centers such as Patrick Ewing, David Robinson and Hakeem Olajuwon, seemed to make much of an impression on O'Neal. Instead

Tom Gugliotta (right) can only watch as Shaq slams home another dunk.

CAREER RECORD

PERSONAL

Birthplace/Date	Newark, NJ/3.6.72
Height /Weight	7–1/315

AWARDS

MVP	None
All-Star Selections	1993–98 (did not play 1997, injured)
Finals MVP	None

CAREER

University	Louisiana State (1989–92)
Pro. Career	6 seasons, Orlando Magic (1992–96), Los Angeles Lakers (1996–98)

PLAYING RECORD	G	FG	Pct	FT	Pct	Reb	Ast	Stl	Bl	Pts	ppg
Regular Season	406	4430	.578	2193	.535	5012	1017	328	1115	11054	27.2
Playoffs	58	596	.579	357	.524	637	199	41	115	1549	26.7
All-Star	5	30	.476	21	.500	38	3	5	8	81	16.2

of feeling his way through the league, O'Neal attacked.

He averaged 23.4 points despite constant double-teams and grabbed an impressive 13.8 rebounds a game. He also

> "I'VE PLAYED WITH MOSES MALONE, DAVID ROBINSON AND KAREEM ABDUL-JABBAR AND I DON'T SAY THIS LIGHTLY, BUT SHAQUILLE'S THE BEST I HAVE EVER PLAYED WITH OR AGAINST."
>
> Mark McNamara, former NBA center

blocked shots, 286 of them in his first 81 professional games to become the easy choice as NBA Rookie of the Year.

"Shaq is much more athletic than I ever thought he would be," says former Orlando coach Matt Guokas. "I played with and against Wilt Chamberlain and Shaq has the same kind of presence on the court. He's the type of force that opposing players always want to be aware of where he is and what he may try to do next. And he can do an awful lot."

Off the court, O'Neal has become the same kind of marketing phenomenon as Michael Jordan. He endorses a wide array of products and already has appeared in a major motion picture. If that's not enough, he is a rap artist with a growing singing career. O'Neal's first album—*Shaq Diesel*—gained critical acclaim and started climbing the record charts from the day it was released.

On the court, the Magic improved from 21 to 41 victories during O'Neal's first season, and to 50 in his second, which O'Neal topped off by being named to the All-NBA Third Team.

Then Orlando and O'Neal really took off. O'Neal won the 1995 scoring title, and led the Magic to 57 wins and a berth in the NBA Finals, where Houston proved just too experienced, sweeping Orlando in four games. Shaq responded to the NBA Finals loss by adding a variety of low-post finesse moves to his arsenal, including a Hakeem Olajuwon-like turnaround jumper. O'Neal took his new bag of tricks with him to the Los Angeles Lakers for the 1996–97 season, setting up shop near Hollywood so he could focus on his budding acting and rapping career. He missed 53 games in his first two years due to injuries, but his presence made the Lakers an immediate title contender.

"He is so big and strong that when you go over to help out on O'Neal, you're taking your life into your hands," says former teammate Horace Grant of Shaquille, whose name means "Little Warrior" in Islam. He's hardly little, but Shaq is definitely a warrior.

O'Neal's incredible size is matched only by his all-around ability, which extends to every corner of the game.

SCOTTIE PIPPEN
Out of the Shadows

There were days growing up in the tiny community of Hamburg, Arkansas, that Scottie Pippen couldn't even play basketball.

It wasn't that there weren't plenty of games going on. It's just that Pippen was considered too small and certainly not good enough to run with his older brothers. So he would stand along the sidelines watching the others play while dribbling a ball and wondering if his time would ever come.

As a high school senior, Pippen was a starting guard with a limited future. He stood only 6–1 and not a single college scout came around to watch him play. His high school coach eventually persuaded a small local college—Central Arkansas—to give Pippen a job helping out with the team, which in turn would help him pay school expenses.

"I was actually a water boy, a manager, on my first college team," says Pippen. "No one thought I could play. Then a couple guys quit the team and I think the coach was tired of hearing me beg for an opportunity. He finally gave me a spot on the team."

Four years later, Pippen had grown to 6–7 and every NBA executive in the country wanted him playing for them. Chicago was one of the first teams to watch Pippen. By the time the 1987 NBA Draft rolled around, the Bulls wheeled and dealed to land him.

After a slow start, Pippen developed into one of the league's most versatile players.

Scottie Pippen orchestrates the play.

CAREER RECORD

PERSONAL	
Birthplace/Date	Hamburg, Arkansas/9.25.65
Height /Weight	6-7/228

AWARDS	
MVP	None
All-Star Selections	1990, 1992–97
Finals MVP	None

CAREER	
University	Central Arkansas (1983–87)
Pro. Career	11 seasons, Chicago Bulls (1987–98)

PLAYING RECORD	G	FG	Pct	FT	Pct	Reb	Ast	Stl	Bl	Pts	ppg
Regular Season	833	5938	.483	2460	.693	5658	4444	1771	765	14987	18.0
Playoffs	178	1186	.449	684	.718	1366	920	344	171	3217	18.1
All-Star	7	34	.442	10	.625	39	17	17	6	85	12.1

Those early days as a point guard had provided Pippen with better-than-average ballhandling skills for a player his size. He could play small forward, substitute for Michael Jordan at shooting guard and, when the Bulls needed a big team on the floor, move over to the point.

By the beginning of the 1990–91 season, Pippen had also developed into one of the league's best defenders. With long arms, unusual quickness, incredible jumping ability and an innate ability to read offenses, Pippen became a defensive force.

"There were times when I felt that Scottie had an even greater potential than Michael," says Bulls assistant coach Tex Winter. "Michael wouldn't agree with that, but Pippen has those long arms and great reaction and he can jump over the moon. Michael could do those things too, but Pippen was a little bigger."

As Pippen developed into a star, the Bulls became champions. Scottie has been an integral part of Chicago's six NBA Championships in the 1990s. He has been a first-team member of the NBA All-Defensive Team for seven straight seasons and was a member of the first and third gold medal-winning Dream Team squads.

Pippen became the prototype for other multi-dimensional players, like Grant Hill and Anfernee Hardaway. Pippen can handle the ball and run an offense like a point guard, hit three-pointers like a shooting guard and post up like a forward—all while playing smothering defense on the opposition's best scorer. While Jordan may be acknowledged as one of the best of all time, Pippen is a deserving choice as one of the NBA's 50 Greatest Players.

....

"THERE WERE TIMES WHEN I FELT THAT SCOTTIE HAD AN EVEN GREATER POTENTIAL THAN MICHAEL [JORDAN]."

Bulls assistant Tex Winter

....

Remark-a-Bull: Scottie Pippen's talents are respected around the league.

DAVID ROBINSON

The Admiral's in Charge

Nicknamed "The Admiral," David Robinson became an All-America center during his four years at the U.S. Naval Academy.

With extraordinary quickness and finesse for a player his size, the 7–1 Robinson reminded NBA coaches of past greats like Bill Russell and Wilt Chamberlain. In fact, some felt Robinson might eventually be the best of them, combining remarkable defensive skills with an offensive game that included everything from dunks to jump shots.

But San Antonio had to wait two years after using the No. 1 pick in the 1987 NBA Draft to select Robinson. Although his height kept Robinson from many military jobs, he was required to fulfill two years of active duty following his final year of school. Robinson was allowed to play in the 1988 Olympics, where he led the men's basketball team to a bronze medal.

"We knew what we were getting," says Bob Bass, the man who drafted Robinson for San Antonio. "We knew what kind of impact he would make on our ballclub. All you had to do was watch him play. There wasn't anything he couldn't do on a basketball floor."

Even after two years off, Robinson became an instant star. He averaged 24.3 points, 12 rebounds and blocked nearly

CAREER RECORD

PERSONAL

Birthplace/Date	Key West, Florida/8.6.65
Height /Weight	7-1/250

AWARDS

MVP	1995
All-Star Selections	1990–96, 1998
Finals MVP	None

CAREER

University	Navy (1983–87)
Pro. Career	9 seasons, San Antonio Spurs (1989–98 — in military service 1987–89)

PLAYING RECORD	G	FG	Pct	FT	Pct	Reb	Ast	Stl	Bl	Pts	ppg
Regular Season	563	5087	.525	4168	.746	6614	1726	940	2012	14,366	25.5
Playoffs	53	445	.488	382	.728	623	156	67	165	1273	24.0
All-Star	7	44	.587	30	.667	50	8	11	11	118	16.9

four shots a game while directing one of the most impressive single-season turnarounds in NBA history. San Antonio finished 21–61 the year before Robinson arrived. With the Admiral in the middle, the Spurs improved to 56–26 and extended Portland to the seventh game of the Western Conference Semifinals, a game the Trail Blazers won in overtime.

"You look at David Robinson and what is there that he can't do?" says Chicago star Michael Jordan. "He's as fast as any big man in the game, he can block shots better than any player in the league and he can score. If he ever develops a sky-hook like Kareem Abdul-Jabbar did, David Robinson will be unstoppable."

But Robinson's greatest season might have been the 1994–95 campaign. He averaged more than 28 points and 11 rebounds per game while leading the Spurs to a franchise-record 62 victories. Unsurprisingly, he was named the NBA's Most Valuable Player for the first time in his career.

And in 1992, Robinson finally got the Olympic gold medal that had eluded the United States in 1988. Robinson was a key member of USA Basketball's Dream Team, as he was again in 1996.

After missing all but six games in 1996–97 with injuries, Robinson came back strong in 1997–98. Teamed with young star Tim Duncan in the middle, Robinson adjusted his game to a "twin towers" approach. This meant sacrificing some of his individual numbers, but that meant little to Robinson. The consummate team player, he lacks only one accomplishment: winning an NBA Championship. At age 33, the Admiral is ready to pull rank on the rest of the league.

The Admiral: Former U.S. Naval officer David Robinson now directs a floor show in San Antonio; OPPOSITE Jump shots are just part of the repertoire.

"DAVID ROBINSON CAN BE AS GOOD AS HE WANTS TO BE IN THIS GAME. HE HAS EVERYTHING IT TAKES TO BECOME ONE OF THE GREATEST CENTERS TO EVER PLAY THE GAME."

Chuck Daly, Dream Team coach

JOHN STOCKTON

No Passing Fancy

John Stockton has never understood all the fuss. As a high school sophomore, Stockton stood 5–4 and weighed just 115 pounds. That he often destroyed players bigger and stronger on neighborhood basketball courts surprised everyone but Stockton.

Somehow John Stockton knew exactly where he was going. More than anyone else, Stockton knew nothing would get in his way, including the pint-size body that housed the spirit of a fighter. But even when the Utah Jazz made Stockton their No. 1 pick in the 1984 Draft, there were skeptics.

How could a player from a small Catholic college called Gonzaga make it in the NBA? And how could anyone standing just 6–1 and weighing less than 180 pounds hope to survive the rough-and-tumble ways of professional basketball?

"I just always thought I could compete," says Stockton simply. "Not that I thought I was better than Magic Johnson or players like that. But I knew I could compete with them."

And that, Utah coach Jerry Sloan will tell you, is exactly why Stockton has become one of the greatest point guards in basketball history. Before Stockton only two players had handed out more than 1,000 assists in a season. Isiah Thomas and Kevin Porter each did it one time. Starting with the 1987–88 season, Stockton dished out more than 1,100 assists for five straight seasons.

CAREER RECORD

PERSONAL

Birthplace/Date	Spokane, Washington/3.6.62
Height /Weight	6-1/175

AWARDS

MVP	None
All-Star Selections	1989–97
Finals MVP	None

CAREER

University	Gonzaga (1980–84)
Pro. Career	14 seasons, Utah Jazz (1984–98)

PLAYING RECORD	G	FG	Pct	FT	Pct	Reb	Ast	Stl	Bl	Pts	ppg
Regular Season	1126	5438	.520	3691	.823	2999	12713	2620	226	15238	13.5
Playoffs	147	719	.480	511	.812	482	1521	278	42	2047	13.9
All-Star	9	30	.492	4	.667	17	69	15	1	71	7.9

Until Stockton only Boston Celtics great Bob Cousy had won more than three consecutive assists titles. Stockton had led the league for eight straight seasons in 1994–95. Until Stockton, superstar Magic Johnson had the highest career average for assists per game with 11.35. Stockton's is at 11.5.

The three highest single-season assist totals in NBA history belong to Stockton, as do the two highest single-season averages. He has had 28 assists in one game and twice passed out 11 in a single quarter.

If Stockton were only a remarkable playmaker he would be an All-Star. But he has twice led the NBA in steals, made the NBA All-Defensive Second Team three times, and averaged more than 13 points a game while making 51 percent of his shots, many of those from three-point range.

That's why Stockton has appeared in every All-Star Game since 1989 and he was an easy choice for USA Basketball's 1992 Dream Team.

Stockton has not received as much notice for his play as he might have if he played somewhere other than Utah, but his record speaks quite loudly. He has become the NBA's all-time leader in assists and steals, and he led the league in assists for nine straight seasons. These numbers earned him a well-deserved spot on the list of the 50 Greatest Players in NBA History.

Stockton led Utah into the national limelight by guiding the team to the 1997 and 1998 NBA Finals. Each time, the Jazz were within two games of victory before falling to the Chicago dynasty. Having had two tastes of the NBA Finals, Stockton hopes to savor an NBA Championship before the end of his brilliant career.

"HE DOES SO MANY THINGS SO WELL THAT TO TRY TO COMMENT ON EACH OF THEM WOULD BE TOO MUCH WORK. LET'S PUT IT THIS WAY, HE'S PERFECT—AND HE'S IMPROVING."

Utah Jazz President Frank Layden

LEFT: Crafty and creative, John Stockton always finds a way to get the ball to his open teammates. RIGHT: Stockton leads the quick break as well as anybody and his partnership with Karl Malone is as good as it gets in the NBA.

RISING STARS

SHAREEF ABDUR-RAHIM
VANCOUVER GRIZZLIES

The Vancouver Grizzlies drafted big Bryant Reeves with their first-ever pick. When their second NBA Draft came around, they picked big again—but they got a dramatically different player.

Where Reeves is a big body with a lot of strength, Shareef Abdur-Rahim is another story. Abdur-Rahim, known to his teammates as "Reef," has the skills of a small forward in the body of a power forward. At 6–10 and 230 pounds, he runs the court like someone six inches shorter, but he makes his presence felt inside.

Abdur-Rahim is part of the new breed of athletic power forwards like Minnesota's Kevin Garnett. He had an immediate impact for the Grizzlies, twice being named NBA Rookie of the Month, playing in the Schick Rookie Game, earning a spot on the NBA All-Rookie First Team and ended his first season averaging 18.7 points and 6.9 rebounds per game, including one triple-double. He showed continued improvement in his second season, impressing observers with his workmanlike attitude and willingness to sacrifice his game for the good of his team.

"I don't care if I play small or power forward. It isn't about what I want," Abdur-Rahim says. "It depends on what the team needs on that given night."

Fitting for a man whose first name means "noble" and last name means "servant of the most merciful one."

KOBE BRYANT
LOS ANGELES LAKERS

After Kevin Garnett's successful leap from high school to the NBA, more teenagers were hoping to bypass college and go straight to the pros. Kobe Bryant was the first to follow Garnett's example, but he had an NBA background: he is the son of a former NBA forward, Jellybean Bryant. After a stellar high school career, Kobe felt he was worthy of the NBA. He had to prove it, however, on the court.

"I didn't know I was ready for the NBA until I stepped on the court and played my first couple of games," Bryant admits.

He was ready. The 6–6 swingman became a key player for the Los Angeles Lakers as the 1996–97 season wore on. He played point guard, shooting guard and small forward, and his 7.6 points per game made for a respectable rookie season.

Bryant truly arrived in his second season, being voted by fans to start the NBA All-Star Game despite not even being a starter for the Lakers. Some feel Bryant is "Air Apparent" to Michael Jordan. Regardless of comparisons, Bryant will be a delight to watch for many more NBA seasons.

TIM DUNCAN
SAN ANTONIO SPURS

San Antonio Spurs fans hope good things are worth waiting for. David Robinson had a two-year naval commitment to fulfill before he could join the team. Tim Duncan, who would have probably been the No. 1 pick in the NBA Draft had he entered it in 1995 or '96, stayed in school at Wake Forest through his senior year. That gave the Spurs a chance to draft him in 1997 with the first pick, creating a twin towers lineup with center Robinson.

Duncan is a natural center, standing 6–10, but he can play power forward next to Robinson. Either way, he saw a lot of playing time as a rookie.

"People are asking me if we'll bring him along slowly," said Gregg Popovich, coach of the Spurs, before the season. "No way. He'll be out there on the court with David and the rest of the starters from day one."

Duncan has all the necessary tools for NBA stardom. And from day one, Duncan showed that he belonged on the court. He was named to the Western Conference All-Star team and averaged more than 21 points and nearly 12 rebounds per game. This effort earned him the NBA Rookie of the Year award, serving notice that Duncan was well worth the wait.

Kobe Bryant (with ball) shows some flashy "O".

Straight to the top: 1998 NBA Rookie of the Year Tim Duncan (21) makes it look so easy.

MICHAEL OLOWOKANDI
LOS ANGELES CLIPPERS

Most NBA players have been dreaming about playing in the league since the first time they ever played basketball. The same is true of Michael Olowokandi — but his first basketball experience came at the age of 18.

Olowokandi was born in Lagos, Nigeria, but grew up in East Sussex, England. And grow he did, topping out at 7–1. Soccer had always been Olowokandi's game, until he picked up a basketball and played with some friends. After a few dunks, Olowokandi decided to learn the game.

"I only played basketball because I was watching NBA videos and I saw all of the fanfare," says Olowokandi. "I saw that and it was something I wanted to be a part of."

At the age of 20 Olowokandi enrolled at University of Pacific, a U.S. college, to better learn the game. Three years later, he was selected by the Clippers with the No. 1 choice in the 1998 NBA Draft.

His game is still raw, but Olowokandi's potential is nearly limitless, and he did aver-age more than 22 points and 11 rebounds per game in his final college season. Olowokandi thinks he's ready to bang big bodies with the NBA's best.

ALLEN IVERSON
PHILADELPHIA 76ERS

Allen Iverson's nickname is "The Answer." The only question NBA fans have for him is "What's next?"

In his first season as a Philadelphia 76er, Iverson was named NBA Rookie of the Year. He put any doubts about his ability to rest with a sizzling five-game stretch in which he scored at least 40 points per game. The high point was a 50-point outburst against the normally stingy defense of the Cleveland Cavaliers.

Iverson's signature move is the crossover dribble, which allows him to blow by uncertain defenders. "I get the guy thinking I'm going one way and I bring it back the other," says the ever-confident Iverson. "The most important thing about dribbling is keeping the ball low and away from the defender."

Not many defenders could keep up with Iverson, who averaged 23.5 points and 7.5 assists per game in his rookie season despite standing only 6–0. He raised eyebrows with his confident on-court attitude, but Iverson backed it up. He even faked Michael Jordan into falling for his crossover move.

Iverson's game is a combination of Jordan's moves with startling speed up and down the court. Comfortable bombing away from the outside or penetrating into the lane and finishing with an explosive dunk, Iverson should be confounding defenders for years to come.

And success-starved Philadelphia fans hope that Iverson will be supplying the answers to their prayers for NBA glory in the near future.

RON MERCER
BOSTON CELTICS

When the Boston Celtics took Ron Mercer in the first round of the 1997 NBA Draft, it was a fitting pick in more ways than one. Not only did it reunite Mercer with his college coach, Rick Pitino, but Mercer and Boston both have a winning tradition.

While at Kentucky, Mercer and Pitino were a part of an NCAA Championship team. When Pitino left Kentucky to coach Boston, he spoke little of the possibility of drafting Mercer, who left the Wildcats as a sophomore. Pitino didn't want other coaches to know how good he thought the 6–7 swingman could be in the NBA.

Once he suited up in the Celtics' green and white, Mercer was a secret no more. His athletic style was a perfect fit for the NBA game, and he went on to average 15.3 points per game in his first season, making the NBA All-Rookie Team in the process.

Mercer's debut was auspicious. His first game was against the Bulls, and his assignment was to check Michael Jordan. Jordan scored 30, but Mercer held him in check down the stretch and added 11 points of his own as the Celtics shocked the defending NBA champs. With his dazzling dunks and gravity-defying moves, Mercer carries the hopes of Boston on his shoulders.

"I ended up where I really wanted to be," he said. "Kentucky has great tradition and the Celtics have the highest level of tradition."

ALL-STAR WEEKEND

It started as an idea. With the NBA trying hard to find its way into the hearts and minds of sports fans, why not gather the league's best players every year for an All-Star Game? In the 33 years between 1951 and 1983, the idea turned into an event as big as any in professional sports. Games were sold out quickly, fans gathered around televisions to watch the proceedings live and players worked to become among the few chosen to participate. Since 1984, the game has been included as part of a gala All-Star Weekend devoted to basketball, complete with additional skill competitions and entertainment for fans of every age.

What began as a game has begotten an entire weekend. At first, the NBA All-Star Game was a chance for basketball fans to watch the league's best players go head to head for 48 minutes. The popularity of the All-Star Game, however, grew beyond that of a curiousity. In 1984, after 33 All-Star Games, NBA All-Star Weekend was born, giving fans the biggest basketball spectacle the game had ever seen.

The game itself is still the focal point of All-Star Weekend, but there is now a three-day festival to whet fans' appetites. As with the game itself, All-Star Weekend is hosted by a different NBA city each year. 1997's event was held at Cleveland's Gund Arena, while the 1998 edition called New York's Madison Square Garden home.

For the fans, All-Star Weekend starts on Thursday with the opening of The NBA All-Star Jam Session. The first Jam Session was held in 1993 at NBA All-Star Weekend in Utah. It has since appeared at Minneapolis, Phoenix, San Antonio and Cleveland. The 1998 Jam Session that overtook New York had more than 400,000 square feet jampacked with interactive basketball fun for the whole family.

Jam Session gives fans the chance to get into the game—literally. If you've ever wanted to hoist a three-pointer, throw down a slam dunk or drain a free throw, Jam Session provides the opportunity. There are also less traditional basketball competitions for fans, like shooting from a trampoline or trying to dunk while attached to a bungee cord.

There's also a chance for fans to see how they stand up to NBA players as physical specimens. Fans can compare their shoe sizes, hand sizes, heights and wing spans with those of NBA players. Jam Session also includes interactive trivia games and a collectibles show. Jam Session runs all the way through NBA All-Star Weekend, giving fans of all ages three days to soak in all the fun.

NBA All-Star Weekend kicks into high gear on Saturday. In the morning the NBA Stay In School Jam takes to the court. This rally for young fans reinforces the importance of a good education. It also serves up great entertainment, with music stars like Boyz II Men and Brandi as past performers. There are also appearances by All-Star players and an entertaining slam dunk contest between the mascots from NBA Teams. One memorable highlight was when the Phoenix Suns' mascot, the Gorilla, dunked after sliding down a rope from the arena rafters.

"The NBA Jam Session presented by Fleer is an integral component of the activities that surround the All-Star Weekend," said Ski Austin, Senior Vice President, NBA Events & Attractions. "The Javits Center is a first-class facility that will be the perfect host for an event of this magnitude."

NBA All-Star Saturday continues with a thrilling evening of basketball. A relatively new wrinkle is the Schick Rookie Game, in which the league's top rookies are divided by

AT&T Long Distance Shootout Champions

1986	Larry Bird, Boston
1987	Larry Bird, Boston
1988	Larry Bird, Boston
1989	Dale Ellis, Seattle
1990	Craig Hodges, Chicago
1991	Craig Hodges, Chicago
1992	Craig Hodges, Chicago
1993	Mark Price, Cleveland
1994	Mark Price, Cleveland
1995	Glen Rice, Miami
1996	Tim Legler, Washington
1997	Steve Kerr, Chicago
1998	Jeff Hornacek, Utah

Nestlé Slam-Dunk Champions

1984 — Larry Nance, Phoenix
1985 — Dominique Wilkins, Atlanta
1986 — Spud Webb, Atlanta
1987 — Michael Jordan, Chicago
1988 — Michael Jordan, Chicago
1989 — Kenny Walker, New York
1990 — Dominique Wilkins, Atlanta
1991 — Dee Brown, Boston
1992 — Cedric Ceballos, Phoenix
1993 — Harold Miner, Miami
1994 — Isaiah Rider, Minnesota
1995 — Harold Miner, Miami
1996 — Brent Barry, L.A. Clippers
1997 — Kobe Bryant, L.A. Lakers

Wham, bam, thank you slam: the Lakers' Kobe Bryant combined power and showmanship to win the 1997 Nestlé Slam-Dunk Championship.

2ball as a way of learning fundamental basketball skills.

THE SELECTION PROCESS

The biggest hand of NBA All-Star Saturday comes when the Eastern and Western Conference All-Star Teams are announced to the crowd. The fans love this part of the show, since they are responsible for picking the teams.

Ballots are made available to fans at games, selected retail outlets and on the NBA's Internet site, NBA.com. Fans vote for five players—a center, two forwards and two guards—they want to start for each conference. Players receiving the most votes then make up the starting lineups for each team. Reserves are chosen by the respective head coaches, who are determined by the top regular season records. The coach of the team with the best record in each conference through the first three months of the current season earns the right to coach that conference's All-Star team.

On All-Star Sunday the teams take to the court and get down to business. During the NBA All-Star Game, the floor often seems more like a stage. Not only are the game's best players rested and ready for action, but they are surrounded by stars at every position. The result is usually a high-scoring game revolving around an array of slick passes, slam dunks and long-range jumpers.

The NBA All-Star Game has become one of the world's biggest sporting events. Reporters from around the globe converge on the event, which is televised worldwide. Sellout crowds and fan frenzy surround the game, providing a fitting climax to a weekend-long celebration of the NBA and the game of basketball.

conference for a fast-paced game. The 1998 NBA Rookie Game was dominated by Cleveland's Zydrunas Ilgauskas, who was named the game's MVP en route to leading the East to an 85–80 win.

There are two additional competitions to excite the fans on NBA All-Star Saturday. The AT&T Long Distance Shootout—first contested in 1986—pits the league's best three-point shooters against each other. Larry Bird won the first three Long Distance Shootouts. Bird started the competition by telling his opponents that they were all playing for second place. Competitors shoot five three-pointers from five different positions around the three-point line. Each basket is worth one point with the exception of the fifth ball at each location—the money ball—which is worth two points. The Long Distance Shootout has been won four times by a Chicago Bull—three times by Craig Hodges and once by Steve Kerr.

The 1998 NBA All-Star Weekend in New York saw a new event add to the excitement. Nestlé Crunch NBA 2ball pairs a player from an NBA team with a WNBA player from the same city. The players alternate shooting from their choice of seven locations on the floor over the course of 60 seconds. Each location is worth a different point value, from two to eight, depending on its distance from the basket. Houston, represented by Clyde Drexler and Cynthia Cooper, outgunned the Utah twosome of Karl Malone and Tammi Reiss for the inaugural NBA 2ball title. Hundreds of thousands of youngsters around the world have played NBA

THE NBA DRAFT

The evolution of the NBA Draft has matched that of the league itself. In the early days, teams gathered around a table in their offices and called off the names of the players selected on a conference call as an official at the league's New York headquarters recorded the information. Few teams did extensive scouting. In the years since, however, the draft has become one of the NBA's biggest shows. Every team studies films, scouting reports and pages of vital information on players from all over the world. The draft itself is now an internationally televised event with 20,000 fans or more packing arenas every year to watch the future unfold.

No one event can change the direction of a franchise quite like the NBA Draft. In the early years as the league evolved, luck and intuition filled the void for teams that didn't have either the money or personnel to scout college players.

In 1955, Leonard Koppett, a veteran basketball writer, described that year's draft session in a column for the *New York Post*. NBA Commissioner Maurice Podoloff sat at the head of a table and called off the names of the league's nine teams.

"Since it is a relatively small family in the NBA, with everyone on quite friendly terms these days, there's a good deal of kidding," wrote Koppett.

"So when Fort Wayne's Charley Eckman chose Dick Howard, Boston's Red Auerbach quipped, 'Is that a relative, Charley?'

"'Wife's cousin,' Eckman shot back."

The atmosphere has changed considerably since. In fact, the entire process has changed massively just in the last 10 years.

"Back then teams didn't even have full-time scouts," says Chicago Bulls vice president of operations, Jerry Krause. "You were lucky if you had an assistant coach, much less a scout. No one had the things that are available today. But that didn't mean you couldn't find players. You just had to dig a little more, that's all."

Welcome to the NBA: 1997 No. 1 pick Tim Duncan (left) is greeted by NBA Commissioner David Stern.

However, the draft has always had a very simple mission: to promote competitive balance throughout the league. Teams selected in inverse order of their regular-season records, so the weakest teams were awarded the first shot at available new talent.

In the hope of solidifying franchises, early teams were also allowed a "territorial pick." Each team could select one player from its geographic area to maintain local interest in the professional team. Over the years, however, territorial picks were eliminated. In 1966, the coin flip was introduced to determine the No. 1 pick in the draft. The idea was to maintain integrity in the game since the team with the worst record wouldn't be guaranteed of landing the first choice.

In some cases the coin flip changed the fortunes of entire franchises. In 1969, the Milwaukee Bucks won a coin flip with Phoenix and ended up with Kareem Abdul-Jabbar. Two years later, the Bucks won an NBA championship. Ten years later, the Los Angeles Lakers flipped with Chicago and won the right to choose first. The Lakers selected Earvin "Magic" Johnson and in 1980 won the first of five NBA titles. Phoenix still hasn't won a championship while Chicago didn't win its first until 1991.

THE LOTTERY

To completely take away any incentive a poor team might have for losing games and thus getting into the coin flip, the league instituted the NBA Draft Lottery in 1985. Initially the lottery was used to determine the order of selection for non-playoff teams or the teams owning those picks through trades. The Lottery determined the order for the first round only, and the order for subsequent rounds went in inverse order of regular season records.

The process was further refined in 1990. The Lottery, which included 11 teams due to expansion, was weighted to favor the worst teams. The team with the worst record had 11 chances to land the No. 1 pick. The second worst team had 10 chances and so on. For the 1994 NBA Draft, the lottery system was modified yet again. The luck of the Orlando Magic led to the most recent change. Orlando gained the No. 1 pick in 1992 and selected Shaquille O'Neal. In 1993, the Magic finished one game out of the playoffs. As a lottery team, Orlando had the lowest odds of gaining the top pick again. But

it happened. The Magic had back-to-back No. 1 picks.

In an attempt to further improve the odds for the league's worst teams, the new lottery system increases the chance of the team with the worst record getting the top pick from 16.7 percent to 25 percent.

Two other key changes over the years involved players and the length of the draft. Prior to 1971, players could not be drafted into the NBA until their college classes had graduated. In other words, a college junior was not eligible to play in the NBA. That changed when Spencer Haywood filed a lawsuit against the league for refusing to allow him to enter the draft before the expiration of his collegiate eligibility. A year later, underclassmen who demonstrated financial hardship were allowed into the draft. In 1976, the draft was opened to all players with or without financial hardship. To become eligible for the draft, underclassmen had to renounce their remaining eligibility in a letter to the commissioner 45 days prior to the draft. That rule remains in place.

The length of the draft has changed as well. After years with no limits to the number of rounds, the league instituted a 10-round draft in 1974. In other words, each team had 10 opportunities to select players.

The draft was reduced to seven rounds in 1985, three rounds in 1988 and the present two rounds in 1989. Those changes, along with the booming popularity of college basketball and professional game, have turned the NBA Draft into a major international media event.

The NBA Draft can turn a franchise around in a matter of years. When Orlando was doubly lucky in the NBA Draft Lottery in 1992 and '93, the Magic were a struggling expansion team. They selected Shaquille O'Neal in 1992, then traded top pick Chris Webber for Anfernee Hardaway in 1993. Those two picks elevated the Magic to a title contender in a couple of short years.

Subsequent No. 1 picks, such as Milwaukee's Glenn Robinson and Golden State's Joe Smith, have become immediate successes for their teams. The top choice in the 1996 NBA Draft, Philadelphia's Allen Iverson, went on to earn NBA Rookie of the Year honors. The last No. 1 pick to be named Rookie of the Year was Tim Duncan, the top 1997 NBA Draft pick, taken by the Spurs. Teaming with David Robinson in the middle of San Antonio's lineup, the Spurs bounced straight back to the playoffs.

Expectations will also be high for the first player taken in the 1998 NBA Draft, Michael Olowokandi, Nigerian-born but raised in London, England, who will hope to enjoy similar success with the Los Angeles Clippers. The Clippers got lucky in the NBA Draft Lottery despite winning six more games than Denver in 1997–98.

Since draft picks can be traded between teams, the NBA Draft has become one of the league's most important offseason events.

As teams now have entire departments devoted to scouting players, complete with state-of-the-art video equipment and large travel budgets, the NBA Draft is a bigger event than ever.

HITTING THE LOTTERY JACKPOT

YEAR	TEAM	FIRST PLAYER CHOSEN
1985	New York	Patrick Ewing
1986	Cleveland	Brad Daugherty
1987	San Antonio	David Robinson
1988	Los Angeles Clippers	Danny Manning
1989	Sacramento	Pervis Ellison
1990	New Jersey	Derrick Coleman
1991	Charlotte	Larry Johnson
1992	Orlando	Shaquille O'Neal
1993	Orlando	Chris Webber
1994	Milwaukee	Glenn Robinson
1995	Golden State	Joe Smith
1996	Philadelphia	Allen Iverson
1997	San Antonio	Tim Duncan
1998	Los Angeles Clippers	Michael Olowokandi

THE NBA GOES GLOBAL

For much of its existence, the NBA remained an American enterprise. But now, with television contracts in more than 160 countries and offices around the world, the league is beginning to make the NBA experience an international one. It started with the McDonald's Championship, an international tournament that featured one NBA team. Now there are 3-on-3 World Tours sponsored in part by Converse, NBA players competing in the Olympic Games and the World Championship of Basketball, expansion to Canada, regular season games played in Japan, and the biennial McDonald's Championship now features the NBA Champion against other club champions from around the world.

The NBA is hardly confined to the United States. After all, the league does have a pair of teams in Canada now. But the NBA's international impact goes far beyond Toronto and Vancouver. The NBA has truly become a global sport with a strong presence in Europe, Japan and Mexico.

Basketball has been gaining steam as a global sport for years, and the NBA's stars were a large part of the game's explosion. The first step was the establishment of the McDonald's Championship in 1987 as a joint venture between FIBA and the NBA. Held every other year, the McDonald's Championship pits the current NBA champs against top teams from around the world. In 1997, the Chicago Bulls earned the chance to represent the NBA against teams from Argentina, France, Greece, Italy and Spain in a six-team tournament in Paris.

The NBA brand of basketball also took center stage in a major way in the 1992 Olympics. For the first time, the U.S. fielded a team of NBA stars rather than collegiate players. The squad was known as the Dream Team, and it was aptly named. The roster included many of the greatest players ever to lace up a pair of sneakers, such as Michael Jordan, Magic Johnson, Larry Bird and Charles Barkley, all coached by the legendary Chuck Daly.

The Dream Team smashed all competition it faced, but the team's victims were glad just to be on the same court with such a legendary bunch—some opponents even asked for autographs before the start of games. By the close of the 1992 Olympic Games in Barcelona, Spain, the world had gotten a large taste of the NBA's style of play.

Two subsequent Dream Teams have continued the mission of spreading basketball around the world. The second such team clobbered the competition at the World Championship of Basketball in Toronto in 1994, while the third Dream Team again won Olympic gold, this time in Atlanta. There the torch was passed to a younger generation of NBA stars such as Grant Hill, Shaquille O'Neal, Anfernee Hardaway and Gary Payton, players the international audience had already learned to love thanks to the fact the NBA now receives television coverage all around the world.

"Since the impressive performance of the Dream Team at the Olympic Games, basketball has gained unprecedented worldwide attention, especially among young people," says NBA Commissioner

Robert Horry at the McDonald's Championship.

David Stern. The NBA has branched out beyond fielding teams for international competition. The league also sends its teams around the world to play in exhibition games.

New York's Patrick Ewing explains the finer points of dribbling to a child on the NBA's Goodwill Tour of Africa in 1994.

In 1998, the Miami Heat traveled to Tel Aviv, Israel, to play Maccabi Tel Aviv, a top Israeli team. It was the first time the NBA has traveled to Israel.

Before the game Shimon Mizrahi, president of Maccabi Tel Aviv said, "Our club has always been part of Europe's elite, and we are very pleased to face one of the NBA's best teams here in Tel Aviv."

The Heat will return for another pre-season game in Israel prior to the 1998–99 season."

THE McDONALD'S CHAMPIONSHIP

In 1997, the Chicago Bulls earned the chance to represent the NBA against teams from Argentina, France, Greece, Italy and Spain in a six-team tournament in Paris. Other NBA teams to have taken part in the McDonald's Championships are the Denver Nuggets, New York Knicks, Los Angeles Lakers, Phoenix Suns and Houston Rockets.

The NBA has also taken steps toward establishing a presence in Mexico. The Dallas Mavericks and Houston Rockets played a regular-season game at Mexico City's Palacio de Deportes in 1997, and 1998 will find the San Antonio Spurs and Los Angeles Clippers doing the same.

"This was terrific," said Charles Barkley after the Rockets' game in Mexico. "You get an opportunity to see your other fans, and they were very supportive of our team. They had energy and enthusiasm throughout the game. It was a fun night."

Prior to these games, Japan has been the only country outside of the U.S. and Canada to host NBA regular season games. In 1990, the NBA became the first American professional sports league to conduct regular season games outside America and Canada when the Phoenix Suns and Utah Jazz opened the 1990–91 season with two games in Tokyo. Games have also been played in Japan in 1992, '94 and '96.

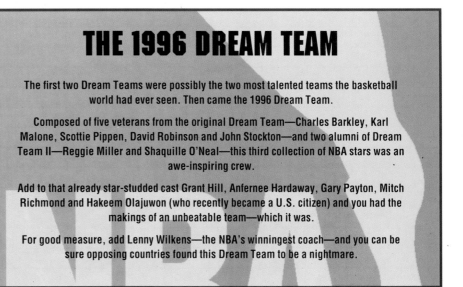

THE 1996 DREAM TEAM

The first two Dream Teams were possibly the two most talented teams the basketball world had ever seen. Then came the 1996 Dream Team.

Composed of five veterans from the original Dream Team—Charles Barkley, Karl Malone, Scottie Pippen, David Robinson and John Stockton—and two alumni of Dream Team II—Reggie Miller and Shaquille O'Neal—this third collection of NBA stars was an awe-inspiring crew.

Add to that already star-studded cast Grant Hill, Anfernee Hardaway, Gary Payton, Mitch Richmond and Hakeem Olajuwon (who recently became a U.S. citizen) and you had the makings of an unbeatable team—which it was.

For good measure, add Lenny Wilkens—the NBA's winningest coach—and you can be sure opposing countries found this Dream Team to be a nightmare.

GLOSSARY OF TERMS

Airball: When a player shoots a shot that doesn't touch the rim it is sarcastically referred to as an "airball."

Alley-oop pass: The pass is thrown as a player runs toward the basket. The receiving player catches the ball in the air and either dunks or lays it in the hoop without touching the ground.

Assist: A player earns an assist when his pass to another player leads directly to a basket.

Backcourt: As it refers to players, backcourt generally means guards. A team with a great backcourt would have two very talented guards.

Bench: Where substitutes and coaches reside during games. A "bench" player is another term for a reserve.

Bounce pass: Passing the ball from one player to another by bouncing it on the floor.

Center: Usually the tallest player on a team's starting unit with a variety of skills that sometimes include shotblocking, rebounding and scoring. New York's Patrick Ewing, San Antonio's David Robinson, the Los Angeles Lakers' Shaquille O'Neal and Miami's Alonzo Mourning are examples of top-flight centers.

Draft: A selection process to determine on which NBA teams the top newcomers will play.

Dunk: The act of slamming the ball through the basket with one or two hands.

Fast break: A play that occurs when the offensive team quickly gets the ball out ahead of the defensive team. The offensive team usually has a one- or two-man advantage as it goes in for a score.

Field goal: Either a two-point or three-point basket can also be referred to as a field goal.

Foul: A violation commited by one player against another player. After accumulating six personal fouls in a game, a player is disqualifed for the rest of the game.

Free throw: When a foul is committed, the player fouled usually gets to take two shots from the free-throw line, which is 15 feet from the basket. The free throws are worth one point each.

Frontcourt: As it refers to players, frontcourt usually means forwards and centers.

Halftime: The time in between the first half and the second half. Each half consists of two 12-minute quarters. Teams break between the second and third quarters and change the baskets at which they shoot.

Jump shot: A shot taken away from the basket. Players usually jump into the air, set themselves and take the shot. Sometimes referred to as a "jumper."

Lane: The painted area running from the end line under the basket out to the free-throw line. Offensive players cannot be in the lane more than three seconds.

Lottery: The process that determines the order of selection at the start of the NBA Draft.

Overtime: When a game is tied at the end of regulation play the two teams play a five-minute overtime period. A game can include as many overtime periods as are necessary to determine a winner.

Paint: The area under the basket, and extending to the foul line. Also called the "lane," it is always painted a different color from the rest of the floor.

Pivot: This takes place when a player who is holding the ball steps and turns once or more than once in any direction with the same foot, while the other foot—called the pivot foot—is being kept at its point of contact on the floor.

Point guard: Usually a team's primary ballhandler. He leads the offense and distributes the ball to the team's best scorers. Phoenix's Kevin Johnson, Orlando's Anfernee Hardaway, Utah's John Stockton and Seattle's Gary Payton are some of the league's best point guards.

Power forward: Usually occupies one of two forward spots on a five-man unit. Known primarily for their rebounding and defensive skills. Utah's Karl Malone, Orlando's Horace Grant and Washington's Chris Webber are examples of power forwards.

Quadruple-double: Refers to a player who accumulates 10 or more in at last four of five statistical categories—points, rebounds, steals, blocked shots, assists—in a single game. Through the 1995–96 season, there have been only four quadruple-doubles in NBA history.

Rebound: The gathering or controlling of a missed shot.

Screen: This is a legal action of a player who, without causing undue contact, delays or prevents an opponent from reaching a desired position.

Shot clock: The 24-second clock used to time possessions. The offensive team has 24 seconds in which to get off a shot.

Shooting guard: Occupies one of two guard positions and usually is one of the team's primary offensive weapons. Chicago Bulls star Michael Jordan is a shooting guard. Others include Indiana's Reggie Miller, Golden State's Latrell Sprewell and New York's John Starks.

Sixth man: Usually refers to a team's top reserve.

Small forward: Occupies one of two forward spots, the small forward is most often known for his scoring. Though not necessarily smaller in size, these players are better known for shooting and scoring skills than rebounding or defensive skills. Detroit's Grant Hill and Chicago's Scottie Pippen are considered small forwards.

Steal: The action of a defensive player in either taking the ball away from an offensive player or intercepting a pass is known as a steal.

Technical foul: Assessed for a number of violations including fighting, verbal abuse of a referee, a second illegal defense call and flagrant foul.

Triple-double: Refers to a player who accumulates double figures, 10 or more, in at least three of five statistical categories—points, rebounds, steals, blocked shots, assists—in a single game.

Turnover: A play that results in a change of possession with the control of the ball going from one team to the other.

BASKETBALL HALL OF FAME

By 1968, the basketball Hall of Fame was an idea whose time was long overdue. Though a memorial had been agreed upon following the 1939 death of Dr. James Naismith, the game's creator, it took nearly 30 years to make the dream a reality.

The Naismith Memorial Basketball Hall of Fame came alive on February 18, 1968, on the Springfield College campus in Springfield, Mass. In 1985 a modern, three-level structure was built on the banks of the Connecticut River in downtown Springfield, the town where Dr. Naismith first tossed a round ball through a peach basket in 1891.

The Hall of Fame recognizes basketball at every level from high school to the Olympics, amateur and professional. An Honors Committee, composed of 24 members representing various levels of basketball, votes each year on nominees, who need 18 votes to be elected to the Hall of Fame. The first Hall of Fame elections were held in 1959, nine years before a building even existed. Since then there have been coaches, players and individual contributors enshrined as well as four teams.

Two of the most outstanding individuals are John Wooden and Bill Bradley. Wooden was named as a player in 1960 and as a coach in 1972. Bradley, who played for the New York Knicks, was a United States Senator and was inducted in 1982.

The following are brief biographies of all NBA-related players in the Hall of Fame:

Kareem Abdul-Jabbar: 7–2, 267-pound center; born April 16, 1947, formerly known as Lew Alcindor. Attended UCLA; played 20 seasons with Milwaukee Bucks and Los Angeles Lakers. Holds NBA record for seasons, games and minutes played, also points scored, field goals (made and attempted) and blocked shots. Also set single-season record for defensive rebounds (1,111 in 1975–76). Named NBA MVP six times, and 18 times an All-Star.

Nate (Tiny) Archibald: 6–1, 160-pound guard; born April 18, 1948. Attended Arizona Western and Texas-El Paso; played 13 seasons with four teams. First player to lead NBA in scoring (34.0) and assists (11.4) in the same season (1973–74). A six-time All-Star.

Paul Arizin: 6–4, 200-pound forward; born April 9, 1928. Attended Villanova; played 10 seasons with Philadelphia. One of the highest scoring players of his era, from 1950 through the end of 1961–62 season. Nine times an All-Star.

Rick Barry: 6–7, 205-pound forward; born March 28, 1944. Attended Miami. Played 14 professional seasons, 10 of those in the NBA. One of basketball's greatest scorers and shooters. A career 90 percent free-throw shooter, utilizing a distinctive underhanded shooting style. Seven-time All-Star.

Elgin Baylor: 6–5, 225-pound forward; born September 16, 1934. Attended College of Idaho and University of Seattle. Played 14 seasons with the Minneapolis and Los Angeles Lakers. Averaged more than 34 points a game for three straight years in the 1960s. 11-time All-Star.

Nate "Tiny" Archibald is the only player to lead the league in scoring and assists in the same season.

123

Walt Bellamy: 6–10½, 245-pound center; born July 24, 1939. Attended Indiana; played 14 seasons with six teams. Bellamy averaged career highs of 31.6 points and 19.0 in his rookie season. Four-time All-Star.

Dave Bing: 6–3, 180-pound guard; born November 24, 1943. Attended Syracuse. Bing played 12 seasons for three teams; led the league in scoring (27.1) in 1967–68. Seven-time All-Star.

Larry Bird: 6-9, 230-pound forward: born December 7, 1956. Attended Indiana State. Played 13 years with the Boston Celtics. Bird helped to redefine the forward position with a combination of scoring, passing, rebounding and defense. As a player, Bird won three NBA Championships, was a three-time NBA MVP (1984, 1985, 1986) and twice NBA Finals MVP (1984 and 1986). In 1997–98, he won the NBA Coach of the Year Award; it was his first year as a coach (with Indiana). A 12-time All-Star.

Bill Bradley: 6–5, 205-pound forward; born July 28, 1943. Attended Princeton. A Rhodes Scholar, Bradley keyed the Knicks' glory days in the 1960s and early 1970s. A former U.S. Senator. One All-Star Game.

Al Cervi: 5–11½, 155-pound guard; born February 12, 1917. Did not attend college. Nicknamed "Digger," Cervi started professional career in 1937. In military service from 1938 to 1945. Cervi finished his NBA career with Syracuse at age of 36. One of the great early guards, he retired before the All-Star Game was instituted.

Wilt Chamberlain: 7–1, 275-pound center; born August 21, 1936. Attended Kansas. A.k.a. "Wilt the Stilt" and "the Big Dipper," Chamberlain is one of the greatest scorers in NBA history, and the only player to score 100 points in an NBA game. Averaged 50.4 points one season (1961–62) and had 30.1 career average. Played 14 years with three teams. 13-time All-Star.

Bob Cousy: 6–1½, 175-pound point guard; born August 9, 1928. Attended Holy Cross. One of the more dazzling ball-handlers in NBA history, Cousy played 13 seasons for the Boston Celtics and finished career with Cincinnati. Set NBA record leading league in assists eight straight seasons. An All-Star 13 times.

Billy Cunningham: 6–6, 220-pound forward; born June 3, 1943. Attended North Carolina. Played nine NBA seasons with Philadelphia and two in the ABA. Four-time NBA All-Star and legendary leaper. Cunningham could do everything from rebounding to scoring. In the late 1980s Cunningham played a major role in creating the Miami Heat franchise.

Bob Davies: 6–1, 175-pound guard; born January 15, 1920. Attended Franklin & Marshall and Seton Hall. Davies' professional career started in 1946. Played 10 years with Rochester as a scoring guard. Played in the first four All-Star Games.

Alex English: 6–7, 190-pound forward; born January 5, 1954. Attended South Carolina; played 15 seasons with Milwaukee Bucks, Indiana Pacers, Denver Nuggets and Dallas Mavericks. Averaged 21.5 points per game in career; led league with 28.4 in 1982–83. Eight-time All-Star.

Julius (Dr. J) Erving: 6–6½, 200-pound forward; born February 22, 1950. Attended Massachusetts. One of the most acrobatic and creative players in NBA history, Erving became known as "Dr. J." Started in the ABA, playing for the Virgina Squire and New Jersey Nets, before finishing career with Philadelphia. An All-Star every one of his 16 professional seasons.

Walt (Clyde) Frazier: 6–4, 200-pound guard; born March 29, 1945. Attended Southern Illinois. Cool and calm on the floor, Frazier was one of the most versatile guards of his era. Played 13 NBA seasons, the first 10 with New York where he led the Knicks to two championships. A seven-time All-Star

.

Joe Fulks: 6–5, 190-pound forward; born October 26, 1921. Attended Millsaps and Murray State. Known as "Jumpin' Joe," Fulks played eight seasons with Philadelphia. One of professional basketball's greatest scorers in the late 1940s. A two-time All-Star.

Harry Gallatin: 6–6, 215-pound forward/center; born April 26, 1927. Attended Northeast Missouri. Played 10 years, nine with New York. A brilliant rebounder, Gallatin was nicknamed "the Horse." A seven-time All-Star.

George Gervin: 6–7, 185-pound guard; born April 27, 1952. Attended Eastern Michigan. Known as "The Iceman," Gervin was one of the great shooting guards ever to play the game. Deadly with a jump shot or his finger-roll lay-ups, Gervin averaged 26.2 points over his career, led the NBA in scoring four times and holds the record for most points in a single quarter—33.

Tom Gola: 6–6, 205-pound forward; born January 13, 1933. Attended LaSalle. Played 10 seasons with three teams. A versatile player with size, Gola helped make Philadelphia a consistent playoff team from the mid-1950s to the early 1960s. A four-time All-Star.

Gail Goodrich: 6–1, 175-pound guard; born April 23, 1943. Attended UCLA. Goodrich played 14 NBA seasons, earning five All-Star appearances. Goodrich was a starter on the 1972 Los Angeles Lakers team that won the NBA Championship. Goodrich averaged 18.6 points over his career.

Hal Greer: 6–2, 175-pound guard; born June 26, 1936. Attended Marshall. A brilliant scoring guard, Greer played 15 NBA seasons, the last 10 with Philadelphia. Averaged more than 20 points a game first seven seasons in Philadephia. A 10-time All-Star.

Cliff Hagan: 6–4, 215-pound forward; born December 9, 1931. Attended Kentucky. A great scorer, Hagan led St. Louis to the 1958 championship. Finished his professional career in the ABA. A four-time All-Star.

John Havlicek: 6–5, 205-pound forward/guard; born April 8, 1940. Attended Ohio State. Brilliant in every phase of the game, Havlicek played on Boston teams that won eight championships. Nicknamed "Hondo," he was drafted by professional football's Cleveland Browns. A 13-time All-Star.

Connie Hawkins: 6–8, 215-pound forward; born July 17, 1942. Attended Iowa, but left after one year to join ABL. After a period out of professional basketball and two ABA seasons, Hawkins joined Phoenix in 1969. Considered one of the greatest pure talents in history. An All-Star four times.

Elvin Hayes: 6–9, 235-pound forward/center; born November 17, 1945. Attended Houston. Missed just nine games in his 16-year career. As great a scorer as he was a rebounder, Hayes helped Washington to the 1978 title. A 12-time All-Star.

Tommy Heinsohn: 6–7, 218-pound forward; born August 26, 1934. Attended Holy Cross. A rugged scorer and rebounder, Heinsohn helped Boston to eight titles in nine-year career. Later coached the Celtics to two championships. A five-time All-Star.

Bailey Howell: 6–7, 220-pound forward; born January 20, 1937. Attended Mississippi State; played 12 seasons with Detroit Pistons, Baltimore Bullets, Boston Celtics and Philadelphia 76ers. Played on 1968 and '69 NBA Championships teams with Boston. Averaged 18.7 points and 9.9 rebounds per game in his career. Six-time All-Star.

Dan Issel: 6–9, 240-pound forward; born October 25, 1948. Attended Kentucky. Played first six professional seasons in ABA, the last nine with Denver Nuggets. A great shooter and rebounder, Issel averaged more than 21 points a game 11 times. Seven-time All-Star.

Harry (Buddy) Jeannette: 5–11, 175-pound guard; born September 15, 1929. Attended Washington & Jefferson. One of the game's top guards in the late 1930s and 1940s. Won four MVP awards and four championships in two leagues.

Neil Johnston: 6–8, 215-pound forward/center; born February 4, 1929. Attended Ohio State. One of his era's greatest scorers, Johnston averaged more than 22 points a game five straight seasons for Philadelphia in the 1950s. Played minor league baseball. Six-time All-Star.

K.C. Jones: 6–1, 200-pound guard; born May 25, 1932. Attended San Francisco. A defensive specialist, Jones played with Bill Russell in college and then at Boston. Helped lead the Celtics to eight championships in his nine NBA seasons. Later became a highly successful NBA coach.

Sam Jones: 6–4, 205-pound guard, born June 24, 1933. Attended North Carolina College. A key to the Boston dynasty, Jones averaged 17.5 points during 12-year career. Member of 10 championship teams in Boston. Five-time All-Star.

Bob Lanier: 6–11, 260-pound center; born September 10, 1948. Attended St. Bonaventure. One of the greatest centers in NBA history, Lanier played 14 seasons with Detroit and Milwaukee. Averaged more than 20 points a game eight straight seasons. Eight-time All-Star.

Clyde Lovellette: 6–9. 235-pound foward; born September 7, 1929. Attended Kansas. Helped Minneapolis to 1954 title as rookie. Solid scorer and rebounder. Played 11 seasons winning two more NBA championships with the Boston Celtics. A three-time All-Star.

Pete Maravich: 6–5, 200-pound guard; born June 22, 1947. Attended Lousiana State. Nicknamed "Pistol Pete" for his extraordinary shooting and scoring skills, he was a veritable ballhandling marvel. Averaged 24.2 points during a 10-year career with the Hawks, Jazz and Celtics. Four-time All-Star.

Slater Martin: 5–10, 170-pound guard; born October 22, 1925. Attended Texas. Member of Minneapolis teams that won four championships. Later helped lead St. Louis to 1958 title. A seven-time All-Star.

Dick McGuire: 6–0, 180-pound guard; born January 25, 1926. Attended St. John's and Dartmouth. One of the great early point guards. McGuire was nicknamed "Tricky Dick" for his ball-handling and passing skills. Seven-time All-Star.

"Pistol" Pete Maravich drives to another score.

George Mikan: 6–10½, 245-pound center; born June 18, 1924. Attended DePaul. The first dominant center in professional basketball history, Mikan led the Minneapolis Lakers to five championships. The greatest scorer of his era, Mikan averaged 23.1 points over his seven-year NBA career, nine seasons in total. Four-time All-Star.

Earl Monroe: 6–3½, 185-pound guard; born November 21, 1944. Attended Winston-Salem State. One of the flashiest guards ever, Monroe was known as Earl "the Pearl" for his smooth moves. Played on New York title team in 1973. Four-time All-Star.

Calvin Murphy: 5–9, 165-pound guard; born May 9, 1948. Attended Niagara. One of the greatest small players in league history, Murphy could score, pass and shoot as well as anyone in his era. One of the best free-throw shooters (89.2 percent) in history. Played 13 seasons, all with Rockets. Appeared in one All-Star Game.

Bob Pettit: 6–9, 215-pound forward; born December 12, 1932. Attended Louisiana State. A brilliant scorer, Pettit never averaged fewer than 20.4 points during 11-year career. Sixth highest career scoring average (26.4) in history. An 11-time All-Star.

Andy Phillip: 6–2½, 195-pound guard/forward; born March 7, 1922. Attended Illinois. Professional career started in 1947. Played on 1957 Boston Celtics championship team. Five-time All-Star.

Jim Pollard: 6–3½, 190-pound forward; born July 9, 1922. Attended Stanford. Known as for his jumping ability, Pollard helped lead Minneapolis to five championships. Four-time All-Star.

Frank Ramsey: 6–3, 190-pound guard/forward; born July 13, 1931. Attended Kentucky. A key contributor to seven Boston championships, Ramsey shot better than 80 percent from the foul line. One of basketball's best "sixth men" ever.

Willis Reed: 6–9½, 235-pound center; born June 25, 1942. Attended Grambling. A gifted shooter and defender despite his size, Reed led the New York Knicks to two championships. Spent 10-year career with Knicks. A seven-time All-Star.

Arnie Risen: 6-9, 200-pound center; born October 9, 1924. Attended Kentucky State and Ohio State. Risen was one of the first great big men of the NBA's early years, playing 13 seasons through the 1940s and '50s. Risen was a member of the 1951 Rochester and 1957 Boston NBA Championship teams. He was known as a great rebounder who was a three-time All-Star.

Oscar Robertson: 6–5, 210-pound guard; born November 24, 1938. Attended Cincinnati. Played 13 seasons with Cincinnati Royals and Milwaukee Bucks. Robertson was considered the greatest all-around guard of his era. Averaged 30.8 points, 11.4 assists and 12.5 rebounds during 1961-62 season. A 12-time All-Star.

Bill Russell: 6–9½, 220-pound center; born February 12, 1934. Attended San Francisco. Led the Boston Celtics to 11 championships during 13-year playing careers. Averaged incredible 22.6 rebounds a game during his career. A 12-time All-Star.

Dolph Schayes: 6–8, 220-pound forward; born May 19, 1928. Attended New York University. Great at virtually every aspect of the game, Schayes could rebound, score and shoot as well as any player in his era. Played 16 seasons, 15 with Syracuse. An 11-time All-Star.

Bill Sharman: 6–1, 190-pound guard; born May 25, 1926. Attended University of Southern California. One of Boston's key offensive threats during the 1950s and early 1960s. Played on four championship teams. A career 88.3 percent free-throw shooter. Played minor league baseball. Eight-time All-Star.

David Thompson: 6–4, 180-pound guard; born July 13, 1954. Attended North Carolina State. Thompson, one of the most electrifying leapers ever to play the game, was an All-Star four times for the Denver Nuggets. Thompson owns the third highest point total in a single game in NBA history, scoring 73 against Detroit in 1978.

Nate Thurmond: 6–11, 230-pound center; born July 25, 1941. Attended Bowling Green. A solid, if not dominant big man during the 1960s and early 1970s, Thurmond could score, rebound and block shots. Five-time All-Star.

Jack Twyman: 6–6, 210-pound forward; born May 11, 1934. Attended Cincinnati. Played nine of 11 seasons in Cincinnati. One of the era's top scoring forwards, averaged 31.2 points during 1959–60 season. Six-time All-Star.

Wes Unseld: 6–7½, 245-pound center; born March 14, 1946. Attended Louisville. Named Rookie of the Year and Most Valuable Player during 1968–69 season. Spent entire 13-year career with Bullets franchise. A five-time All-Star.

Bill Walton: 6–11, 235-pound center; born November 5, 1952. Attended UCLA. One of the greatest college players ever. Walton led Portland to the 1977 title and helped Boston to 1986 championship. His career was cut short by chronic foot injuries (played in only 14 games in four seasons 1978–82). Played in one All-Star Game.

Bobby Wanzer: 6–0, 172-pound guard; born June 4, 1921. Attended Colgate and Seton Hall. Played 10 years with Rochester. A great free-throw shooter, Wanzer developed into a reliable scorer while leading the Rochester offense to 1951 NBA title. Five-time All-Star.

Jerry West: 6–2½, 180-pound guard; born May 28, 1938. Attended West Virginia. One of the greatest shooting guards in history, West averaged 27.0 points during his 14-year career. He teamed up with Wilt Chamberlain to lead Los Angeles to the 1972 NBA championship. A 12-time All-Star.

Lenny Wilkens: 6–1, 185-pound guard; born October 28, 1937. Attended Providence. One of the game's smartest point guards, Wilkens started his coaching career while still a full-time player. An All-Star nine times during his 15-year playing career and the NBA's all-time winningest coach, Wilkens is enshrined in the Hall of Fame as a player and as a coach.

George Yardley: 6–5, 195-pound forward; born November 23, 1928. Attended Stanford. In seven NBA seasons, Yardley was named to the All-Star team six times. He became the first NBA player to score 2,000 points in a single season, doing so in 1957–58 for the Detroit Pistons.

INDEX